Three Shoes, One Sock & No Hairbrush

Three Shoes, One Sock & No Hairbrush

REBECCA ABRAMS

CASSELL&CO

To my children,
Jessica and Solomon

*The family is like a little kingdom, and
like most other kingdoms, is generally in
a state of something resembling anarchy*

G. K. CHESTERTON

Contents

INTRODUCTION

Not so very long ago (but also light years away), when having another baby was still just a vague intention, I used to assume that having one child was the best possible qualification for having a second. In fact, what better qualification *could* there be? I knew all about pregnancy, labour and after, didn't I? I'd done pelvic push-ups and aqua-natal classes; I'd done entonox trips and vaginal stitches; I'd done gargantuan bras, hot flannels and nipple creams; I'd done breast-feeding and burping; I'd done broken nights and chronic fatigue; I'd done baby rice and freezer-fulls of nutritious, multi-coloured ice-cubes; I'd done baby gym and mini-maestros; I'd done childcare traumas and going-back-to-work. What more could there possibly be to know?

Only later, when the dreamy notion of 'another baby' had solidified into a set of rapidly multiplying cells due to make an appearance as a fully fledged human being in around nine months' time, did I begin to realise that having one baby was not going to be much of a preparation for a second.

What I fully understood only in retrospect is that every baby is different, and every woman's experience of every baby is different, from conception on. The most fundamental change of all is that second time round, you are not only a pregnant woman, but a pregnant *mother*. And as I rapidly discovered, pregnancy and motherhood are weirdly incompatible. My two-year-old still needed my time and attention and energy, pregnancy or no; her daytime requirements did not go away simply because I had morning sickness; her night-time wakings did not cease simply because I needed more sleep than usual; her clothes still needed washing, her tea still needed cooking. She still needed *me*, in short, and wasn't going to let me off the mothering hook for nine months just so that I could gestate a sibling.

The *in vitro* sibling, meanwhile, had an agenda of its own. It too demanded my attention, sapped my energy, ruthlessly redirected my resources towards its needs over everyone else's. 'I cannot play pirate ships with you right now,' I would try to explain to my daughter, 'because I currently have something inside me called a placenta, and it's doing its stuff, and I'll throw up if I move so much as a little finger.' From her perspective this was not a good excuse.

Throughout the pregnancy I'd clung to the idea that life would return to normal once the baby was born; instead the shocks and surprises continued. My easy-going first baby was succeeded by a decidedly stroppy second baby. She'd been a picky eater whereas he was an all-out guzzler. She'd been a reluctant sleeper while his sleep-pattern was as regular as clockwork. Now that the children are aged six and three, the differences between them are more numerous than ever. And just as significantly, the differences between how I was with just one child and how I am with two also mount up as time goes on. I am more relaxed in some ways, much less so in others; more confident in some ways, more anxious in others. I spend more time tidying up and less time playing, yet I am also more aware of how short these early years of childhood are, and how precious. Having a second child has changed me as a woman and as a mother; it has changed my relationship with my first child, and with my husband; it has affected my health, my social life and my work. The mother-of-two me is not better or worse, but she is most decidedly *different*.

Of all our expectations of parenthood, this is the one that most regularly trips us up: the expectation that having a second child will be pretty much like having a first. Few of us, let's be honest, are even prepared for the fact that our children will *look* different, or have different personalities. Why else do second-time parents spend so much time exclaiming incredulously: 'They're *so-o-o-o* different!'? Nearly every woman I spoke to while researching this book used the same phrase: 'I thought it would be like first time round.' As Judy Dunn puts it in *From One Child to Two*: 'Change is perhaps the only thing you can be certain of, both in what you feel and in the demands that you'll have to face.'[1]

If our first child changes our life, our second child changes it *all over again*. For a start there is the impact on the routines and structures of daily life: getting not one, but two children dressed, fed, washed, bathed; running two children's social lives; monitoring two children's emotional, physical and psychological development. Then there is the impact of the child itself, who can be so unlike the first child in temperament, appearance and aptitude and who will forge an entirely unique bond with each of its parents. The domestic triangle we'd just about got used to has suddenly become a square. We've added a whole new person to the complex structure of family life and – as we soon discover – the entire constellation of familial connections is altered by the new star in its midst. What's surprising is how many of us fail to anticipate these changes in advance; how unprepared we are for the impact of our second child.

One reason for this, quite simply, is lack of information. A plethora of publications, videos, classes and courses await the first-time mother, but the second-time mother is assumed already to know all she needs to know. The first-time mother is accompanied every step of the way on her amazing voyage of discovery, but the second-time mother doesn't even get a rousing send-off. The first-time mother is deluged with information, the second-time mother must navigate her way chiefly on instinct. In short, having a second child is treated as if it were merely a repeat trip, the same familiar journey all over again. Having survived one pregnancy, one labour and one small baby, you're pretty much on your own. Most baby manuals go no further than a few coyly inadequate paragraphs on sibling rivalry. With around 240,000 second babies being born each year in Britain alone, that makes for an awful lot of unprepared mothers.

It is, of course, perfectly true that our first child marks a major – perhaps the major – turning point in our life. That first pregnancy, that first labour, those first weeks and months with a new baby – all unquestionably combine into a profound rite of passage for most women. Sheltered from the daily realities of caring for a small baby until we have one of our own, there is a devastatingly steep learning curve as we suddenly become expert in the social, psychological, medical and environmental needs of the tiny being who has just taken over our world.

But a second child also brings profound and often unanticipated changes. And for a great many women the impact of the second child is as dramatic as it is unexpected. 'It's the big shift,' one mother-of-five told me. 'Having three or four children doesn't make all that much difference, it's just a matter of degrees. But going from one to two is a huge change.'

The repercussions of the shift from one child to two can be seen in almost every area of a woman's life: physically, emotionally, professionally, socially and, of course, financially. For many of us, the second child will create not just ripples, but shock waves. Alongside the profound pleasures and unique rewards of being a mother-of-two, there are also the practical challenges of caring for two children simultaneously and the emotional adjustment to loving two children at once. Gender roles become even more polarised; exhaustion levels can become chronic; marriages often reach crisis point; the economics of working to pay for childcare in order to work become unsustainable, and the logistics of combining working and mothering often start to break down beneath the daily pounding of life with small children. Small wonder that mental health problems peak in mothers of under-fives. It's not just a matter of expanding the family; it's a psychological and practical seismic shift.

As a second child myself, I am naturally in favour of them. As a mother-of-two, I also know that my own second child is an unquenchable source of pride, pleasure and delight. I am as besotted by my boy as any mother could be. His exuberant, tumultuous presence has, without question, expanded the love-and-laughter quotient in our household, but I can't pretend that having a second child has not also brought new complications, tensions and stresses to our lives. Above all else, having a second child is a contradictory experience. Perplexing, taxing and exhausting, but also rewarding, exciting and deeply satisfying. The good and the bad don't cancel each other out, they exist alongside one another: a double-stitch that runs through the minutes and hours and days, so seamlessly that it is impossible to tell the point at which one tips into the other.

From conception on, then, the second child makes a difference, but it's not the same difference that a first child makes. It is the nature of this difference – so little discussed in public, so widely experienced in private – that I explore and write about in this book. In Chapter One, I take a closer look at the transition from one child to two, at why we can often feel so unprepared for the changes our second child brings, and how the images of mothering that surround us, verbally and visually, contribute to this. Chapter Two offers practical information on second pregnancy and labour, including how to prepare your firstborn for the arrival of a sibling. Chapter Three explores one of the most hidden aspects of having a second child: how your feelings for your first child can change in profound and unexpected ways. I also look at the conflicting emotions

One Becomes Two

Here are some of the things other parents have said about becoming and being a mother-of-two:

'It's wonderful having two children – now! But for the first 12 months I didn't know what had hit me. I felt completely overwhelmed.'

'Two is basically much easier than one, because you've already made the big change to your life, not being able to go out when you want, sleep when you want, have sex when you want.'

'Having your second child is like having your first, but without all the worry.'

'I thought it would be like the first time. Nobody told me how different it would be.'

'My marriage was in a bad way, but for some mad reason I persuaded myself that having another baby might bring us closer. I adored my second child right from the start – he was a gorgeous, smiley baby – but the strain of another child was too much for my marriage.'

'I expected to be up and about much more quickly after my first child was born. In fact I was in a worse state and needed longer to recover.'

'The first year or so was unbelievably tiring, but we're through that phase, and now, when I look at my children and see them laughing together about something, or when we're all out as a family at weekends, it's just the most wonderful feeling. Being a mother is a great privilege really. It's hard at times, yes, but the rewards are unbeatable.'

that loving two children at once can often rouse in a mother. In Chapter Four, children's reactions to the arrival of sibling are explained. I suggest a number of practical measures parents can take to reduce the distress to their firstborn and to increase the chances of their children developing a close relationship. Chapter Five goes into the sibling relationship in more detail, exploring issues such as jealousy, aggression and violence between children, as well setting out some golden rules for handling conflict without taking sides. Chapter Six looks at the impact of having two children on the adult relationship and on a woman's sense of her self. Juggling work and home commitments becomes still more of an issue with two children, and in Chapter Seven, I identify a 'Second Child Syndrome' and look at why this is the moment when many women decide to re-evaluate their working lives. Chapter Eight sets out an agenda for pleasurable survival of life with two children. It offers pearls of wisdom and reassuring suggestions from other mothers-of-two.

Whatever else a second child may be, it is never just another child. Whatever else a second child may be, it is never the same as a first child. Whatever your experiences of becoming a mother first time round, the experience second time round will always bring surprises. It is my hope and belief that if we can look steadily and honestly enough at the true mix of experiences that accompany the mother-of-two every step of the way – the joys and the frustrations, the loving and the hating, the gains and the losses – the demands of life with two small children will be easier to endure, the pleasures and rewards easier to relish.

'*Now what?!*'

One

The Transition to Two

It's a dark, rainy November afternoon. We are squeezed – my two-year-old daughter and I – into the changing cubicle of Dorothy Perkins. I am trying on maternity clothes. Though barely pregnant I already feel queasy enough for anything with waistbands to be out of the question. In between garments I feel a small hand reach up and pat my stomach. 'Mummy,' my daughter asks, 'is that a baby in your tummy?' How does she know? There is no bump. I've not yet taken to lying around on sofas looking green. Whatever it is that's given the game away, she knows. I am well aware that the official advice is not to tell your first-born too soon, but it seems pointless to lie. 'Yes, actually,' I say rather sheepishly. 'It is.'

From my side of the bump, the revelation is that the process of becoming a mother-of-two is already underway. The transition has begun and my daughter is as involved as her father and I. When he lays his cheek on the bump to feel it kicking, her peach-plump cheek follows suit. When he puts his lips to the bump and calls 'Hello in there', her high treble joins in. At antenatal check-ups, she likes to have her heartbeat monitored too. She is as busy learning how to be a sibling as I am learning how to be a mother to them both.

How easily a woman makes the transition from mothering one to mothering two will depend on a whole host of factors connected to her past experiences and her current circumstances, but the transition is seldom entirely predictable or straightforward. American psychologists Philip Cowan and Carolyn Cowan have spent the best part of 30 years studying how couples make the transition to parenthood. They set up the 'Becoming a Family Project' in California in 1974 and have been tracking the impact of children on couples ever since. The Cowans discovered that about 50 per cent of couples found having their second child an easier transition than their first; the other 50 per cent found it much harder. Among the women I interviewed for this book, I encountered the same 50:50 split. But the mothers who were finding it easier did not say *every* aspect of having a second child was easier; they said that the *overall* experience was easier. Similarly, those who were finding it harder were still able to identify positive aspects of the experience, even though their dominant experience was of the difficulties of mothering two.

Without exception, all of the women I interviewed, both those who'd sailed through and those who'd struggled along, felt that it had taken time to get used to being a mother-of-two, that there had been a definite period of adjustment. Very few of them had anticipated this in advance.

Mothers are not alone in underestimating the impact of the second child. Very few of the authorities on baby- and childcare describe or analyse the experience of looking after two children at the same time; about loving two children at the same time; about meeting two sets of needs, interests and demands at the same time. No one mentions that one of the most stressful aspects of life with two children, especially at the beginning, is that most of these demands will be conflicting and simultaneous: the baby is screaming to be picked up just as your toddler suddenly and desperately needs to poo; you are breast-feeding the infant and your four-year-old falls off her tricycle; you are reading to your five-year-old when your two-year-old appears in the doorway brandishing the garden shears. In such all-too-common moments you can feel impossibly pulled in different directions and your stress levels, inevitably, soar. These are the run-of-the-mill occurrences in households with small children. The real toll they take, the real stress they cause, are seldom mentioned or discussed. Top of my personal hit list for unhelpful advice, given in many baby books, is the suggestion that new mothers-of-two should read to the older child while breast-feeding the baby. But *how?* You've got one arm round the baby and one arm round the toddler. How are you meant to hold the book, or turn the pages? With your toes?

Given the unrealistic, or simply non-existent, advice that mothers typically receive, it is hardly surprising that many new mothers-of-two are shocked when things don't go that smoothly. 'Most childcare experts write as if a mother is only dealing with one child at a time, when of course that is not usually the case', according to child psychiatrist Dr Anna Graham. 'When mothers find they just can't give their second child the time and attention they gave to their first, many women feel they are failing.'

A study of 40 second-time mothers by psychologists Judy Dunn and Penny Munn found many women worry that they are short-changing their second child, not giving them the quality or quantity of attention that they'd given to their first child at the same age.[1] Even though the researchers couldn't actually *see* any difference between the way the mothers treated their first and second children, the mothers themselves felt they were 'under-performing' with their second child, and they felt bad about it. This was also a common theme with the women I interviewed, many of whom said they guilty about not giving their second child the attention they'd given to their first.

Fiona is 34 and married to Peter, who runs an internet business. They are the parents of six-year-old Phoebe and three-year-old Luke. Fiona articulates the feelings of many: 'I don't do any of the things I used to do with Phoebe at his age. I haven't taken Luke to a single baby group, or swimming, or anything. It's usually mid-morning before I've got us all dressed and then it's too late. Even when we're at home, I spend much less time playing with him and much more time clearing up. Playing with either one of them is hard because the other gets bored or jealous. There doesn't seem to be nearly as much time as there was when it was just Phoebe.'

The Myth of the Mother – One Child

Having cared for one baby already, we may not need to be told how to look after a second *baby*, but what many women badly need is information about looking after *two children*. As another mother put it, 'The baby is easier second time round, but the combination is harder.'

A child will usually have only one mother, but the majority of mothers will find themselves, sooner or later, balancing the needs of more than one child. Most of us grew up in families of more than one child and, as parents, will go on to have families of more than one child. For most families, having one child is just a brief staging-post on the way to having two. Of the 20 or so years that we are engaged in active parenting, most of us will spend just one or two years raising a child on its own. Yet despite the fact that most women who have one child will go on to have another, the books, the research, the magazine articles, the advertisements all carry on as if one child were the norm, while the norm – two children – is treated as an anomaly barely worth mentioning. The transition from being a mother-of-one to a mother-of-two is a hugely significant, and often fraught, time in a woman's life, yet it passes almost entirely unremarked.

The experiences of the second-time mother are overlooked to a quite extraordinary extent in our society. Not only are we surrounded by representations of motherhood that tend to show a mother with a single child, but these images themselves are underpinned by a powerful ideology of mothering that stubbornly revolves around the notion of a one-to-one relationship between a mother and her child – *singular*. The pervasive model of mothering is of mothering *one*. From the moment we conceive our second child, this model of mothering becomes inappropriate, yet it continues to inform our expectations about what mothering two will be like, or ought to be like. However many children joyously crowd around us in our secret fantasies of family life, in our mind's eye we see a competing image: *one* mother caring for *one* child.

Once you start to question the models of mothering on which we base our own mothering selves, it becomes clear that the anxiety that so many women feel about how they mother their children (or rather, how they're *not* mothering them) says very little about people's actual mothering ability and a great deal about inappropriate expectations – and where they come from. The emphasis on the mother-of-one is particularly problematic in an age where mothers look to books and magazines for advice and guidance, but it is not new. For 2,000 years, Christianity has been feeding Western society with images of the Madonna and child, cosily gazing at one another, without so much as a glimpse of Jesus's various siblings, whom history assures us *were* there. It is unlikely that Mary ever indulged in quite such blissfully undistracted moments of adoration, however her son was conceived. Yet that is the image that has become the model for Western mothering ever since, the standardised version to which we all subscribe – at least until real life puts things into a rather different perspective.

After the birth of my second child, I felt out of my depth and very alone. I blamed myself for not coping, watched other, calmer mothers in silent wonderment, pretended in company to a competence I didn't feel, but alone with the children I felt evermore inadequate and overwhelmed, bounced between baby and toddler like an increasingly crazed shuttlecock.

Second children don't just slip quietly into the family stew, they are a whole new and dynamic ingredient. A second child is born into – and creates – a very different family environment from the first. It is often a more complex environment, certainly emotionally, for the simple reason that more people are involved this time round, more relationships have to be taken into account. In addition, all of these people, and the relationships between them are not fixed but continually changing: the issues that second-time parents face in the first three or four weeks, for example, are not the issues they will be facing in the second month, or the sixth.

Most of us do realise in advance that the first week or so after the new baby is born may be a bit testing. We recognise that our first-born may need a little time to get used to having a sibling. Typically, we allow a few days, maybe a fortnight, for making this adjustment, after which time we think we should have learnt the score. For most of us, though, it's not a matter of days or weeks, but months. My own view is that the whole of the first year with two children is often a period of adjustment. Within that year, there are distinct stages and turning points; some of these will make the path even bumpier for a while, others will reveal the light pouring in at the far end of the tunnel. Beyond the first year, the challenges of parenting two children continue and change, but for most people, ordinary, daily life will slowly and steadily start to get easier.

In an ideal world, the transition to two would start *before* our second child is born, not with undignified abruptness in the days and weeks immediately after. Long before we find out whose nose the baby has, and whose temper, the conditions that determine how we will cope are taking shape. A combination of our own personality and circumstances, as shifting as the contours of the Norfolk coastline, will be what makes the biggest difference to our experience of second-time parenthood: a bit of confidence eroded here, a more secure job added there. If only more of us were able to take a moment to cast a long, steady look at our expectations, our past experiences, our current situation *before* our second child was born, we might find ourselves better equipped in the event. Janice, a secondary school teacher in Buckinghamshire, is married to Jonathan, a computer engineer, and they have two children, mother-of-Gareth, five, and Eva, three. 'Looking back on that first year, I think one of the main problems was that I started out with completely unrealistic expectations, and then, once Eva was born, I had no time to think about what was going on. I was too busy surviving!' recalls Janice.

How the Past Can Shape the Present

Expectations are invariably based on past experience, in this sphere of human activity as in every other, and your experience of having your first child will shape your expectations of your second child. A straightforward, intervention-free first labour, for instance, is bound to leave you and your partner feeling more enthusiastic about giving birth for a second time than would a traumatic, high-tech drama. Similarly, if you had a demanding first child, everything after will seem relatively easy. When the difficult baby comes second, however, you are wrong-footed from the start.

If your first child was an easy baby, you may have simply assumed that your second child would be too, but the chance of having an easier second baby is definitely not one to lay bets on. There is no pattern of easiness with babies: their constitutions, gender, personalities are as unpredictable as the day and way of their arrival. An easy first baby may be followed by another easy baby or by a complete shocker. One 'difficult' baby may be followed by another or by a little angel. Studies of first and second children have failed to pinpoint any reliable pattern of difference. What it boils down to is that some second children are easier, some are harder. All we know for sure is that mothers *experience* their children differently.

Often the fact that we have any expectations of our second children at all is a hindrance, since those expectations are invariably based on an entirely different child. And when our second child is also a different sex from our first, such expectations can be particularly irrelevant. Discovering our baby's gender will trigger a particular response within us. For many mothers, the response a baby boy triggers is, at least in part, anxiety. As Steve and Shaaron Biddulph point out in *Raising Boys*: 'Most women say they feel more confident with a baby girl. They feel they would intuitively know what to do with her. But a boy! After the birth of a son, it's not unknown for a mother to exclaim in horror, "I don't know what to do with a boy!" However well prepared we are logically, the emotional response is often still, "Wow! This is unknown territory!"'[2]

There are a number of well-documented differences between infant boys and girls, which taken in total strongly suggest that boy and girl babies need, and evoke, somewhat different care. Infant boys, for example, are often 'harder to settle' – a glorious euphemism – than girls. One explanation for this is that boys are born with less-developed digestive tracts than girls, so suffer more from indigestion and stomach aches and so forth. Infant boys are five times as likely to suffer from a gastric condition named pyloric stenosis, the main symptoms of which are vomiting (often projectile), constipation and weight loss. A number of studies have shown that infant boys spend more time crying, and more time being rocked than infant girls. Boy babies are also less sensitive to touch, take longer to sleep through the night, and are likely to be weaned later. All of which means baby boys can be harder work than girls. Not always, of course, but often. My son was undoubtedly a far more demanding baby than my daughter had been. He loathed being placed in a pram or bouncy chair; rapidly developed an aversion to slings and carriers; had no interest in watching the world go by; instantly detected the moment he was left alone in a room; rarely slept or fed for longer than 20 minutes at a time; and was only ever really content when nuzzled up against a nice, soft, warm, preferably female body. This state of affairs lasted for four months, by which time I was going demented, and so was his two-and-a-half-year-old sister. His seemingly ceaseless demands fuelled my anxiety; my seeming inability to soothe him fuelled it further. No doubt he responded to my anxiety and became more fretful still. When he wasn't fretting he was adorable beyond imagining, but the bad moments were ghastly.

Past experiences can also make the transition to two much smoother than anticipated. 'It is often only with the arrival of a second baby that a woman really feels confident of her ability, and relaxes enough to be able to enjoy those early weeks and months', writes Kate Figes in *Life After Birth*.[3] This was certainly the case with my friend Ruth, a self-employed architect of 38, married to James, a designer, and mother of two girls, Hannah and Rachel. Ruth amazed me one afternoon by announcing, 'It's so much easier second time round, isn't it?' Well, it was going quite nicely at that particular moment. We were sitting in the spring sunshine in her cottage garden with our four children (youngest then aged two) playing contentedly around us. But even so I couldn't believe what I was hearing. Was this the same woman whom I knew had found the pregnancy harder, the labour harder, the breast-feeding harder, who'd had no childcare until her second was eight months old, who'd had low-level viruses for a whole year after her younger daughter was born, who'd been desperately worried about her mother's health, and whose father had almost died? Ruth was adamant: 'I know, I know. All that's true. Some things *have* been harder. But all in all it's been a lot easier.'

For Ruth, the crucial factor that kept the 'easier' side of the scale weighted firmly down was her mental state: 'The biggest difference second time round was that I didn't feel anxious about the baby. With my first, I was so worried the whole time. I worried about car accidents and paint fumes and food additives and toxins in toys. I worried the baby was too cold or too hot, or not getting enough to eat, or getting too much. James got really fed up with me, so there was a lot of strain between us too. By the time I had my second child, I was much more relaxed. Looking after two children was physically more tiring, but there wasn't any of the terrible mental stress I'd had with my first.'

Ruth found that her prior experience of being a mother helped her to be a better mother second time round. She also felt that her experiences of being a child herself contributed to her positive frame of mind with her second child. As the youngest in a family of six children, she had clear memories of her own mother looking after several children at once. Ruth's mother provided her with a strong role model for mothering more than one. With family size shrinking from generation to generation, fewer women today have the kind of memories that Ruth has of her mother. Most of us will not have conscious memories of seeing our mothers caring for several children simultaneously, of juggling different children's needs and wants and tempers and tears. What we are more likely to remember is how we got on with our brothers and sisters, not how our mother managed to get on with all of us.

Fiona is also the youngest of six children, but in her case, her mother had become severely depressed after her fourth child, and the repercussions of this were felt not only throughout her childhood, but reached into Fiona's own experiences of mothering. 'My mother was in and out of hospital throughout my childhood, and I remember some weeks when she couldn't even talk she was so depressed. I have always been afraid that I might go through something similar with my children – it's been like a black cloud always hovering over my head, always cutting out some of the happiness my children have brought me. I wasn't so worried when I had my first child, but the fear seemed to get worse with my second.'

Our relationships with our own parents colour and shape our experiences of parenthood. Becoming a mother can ease or exacerbate tensions with one's own mother. One woman I interviewed, who described her relationship with her mother as 'a lifelong tale of thwarted love', found that their relationship had improved dramatically after the birth of her first child, only to plummet to worse-than-ever depths of frustration and misunderstanding with the birth of her second. Women who have lost their own mothers in childhood or adolescence, whether through death or divorce or illness, will often find the experience of mothering a profoundly ambivalent one. In *Motherless Daughters,* Hope Edelman explains how women who were bereaved in childhood or adolescence can find unresolved grief reawakened when they in turn become mothers. The impact of maternal bereavement in childhood can run down the generations in powerful ways: one of Edelman's interviewees was distressed to find herself 'cutting off' emotionally from her infant daughter. Through therapy, this woman realised that she was re-enacting the experiences, not just of her mother, but also of her grandmother, whose mother had died when she was a baby. Through my own work with bereaved people, I also know that for women whose mothers have died, the experience of becoming a mother themselves helps to forge a mental bond with their own mothers, which can greatly ease their sense of loss.

Past events can influence current experiences in another important way. Most parents will themselves have been or become siblings as children. The relationship they enjoyed or loathed with their siblings may colour their feelings towards their own children at this time. One woman I interviewed had been an adored second child, but her birth had been a devastating blow to her older sister. She and her sister had fought continually as children, and she had often suffered from her sister's jealous bullying and unprovoked attacks. As her second pregnancy advanced she began to dream repeatedly about her sister. She became increasingly anxious about how her first child, a girl, would react to the new baby, worried that she was somehow about to inflict on her beloved child the misery she had, albeit unintentionally, caused her sister. Even after the baby was born, she found it hard not to feel highly protective of her first-born, and it was many months before she began to feel affectionate and tender towards her second child.

Smoothing the Transition from One to Two

Past experiences, as a child, sibling and parent, all play an important part in shaping your conscious and unconscious expectations about having a second child. On top of this, your current circumstances will have a critical role in how you personally experience the transition from one to two. Are you happy where you live? Is there anywhere to go with the children during the day? Have you enough money? Are you still with your children's father? Are you planning to go back to work at some stage? Is your job secure? Is your partner's job secure? Can you afford to pay for two lots of childcare? How have you recovered from giving birth second time round? How involved is your partner with the children? How often do you get to see close friends? Do you have any relations living close by?

Too much additional stress in other areas of your life will also make it harder to adjust to a new baby, so try to keep other sources of stress to a minimum. This won't always be possible, of course. Janice's mother died of liver cancer eight months after the birth of her second child, Eva. 'I was very close to my mother and she died very quickly after being diagnosed. It was a terrible shock. The worst thing was that there was no time or space to grieve for her. I was so busy with the children and I had to keep going for them – perhaps that was a good thing, but I also found myself resenting their demands. I took a lot of my anger out on my husband. Our relationship was very strained for about six months after she died.'

While we can't timetable death and illness, it's extraordinary how many of us manage to introduce stress into our lives quite unnecessarily. We've got a newborn baby, a cheesed-off toddler, a neglected spouse. We haven't slept more than two hours at a stretch for weeks. The washing machine is overflowing and the fridge is a wasteland. We need extra stress like we need a blocked lavatory. Do we do the sensible thing? No, we go ahead and make major changes to our lives anyway. Thus there is an immutable law of parenthood predicting that 90 per cent of those parents who resist the urge to move house just before or just after the birth of their first child will do so just before or just after the birth of their second. It's bizarre, irrational and idiotic, but we all do it. I did it. My only advice on house moves and second children is: DON'T DO IT. Resist the temptation. Quash the urge. Say to yourself several hundred times a day: 'Moving house requires more energy, time and money than 14 children put together.'

Whatever your circumstances, support is a major – perhaps *the* major – buffer to stress for women at home with small children. We need support at this stage in our lives, from our partner, from family and friends, from colleagues and neighbours, and, if necessary, from health visitors and GPs. For the couples in the American studies described earlier, support took the form of a group of strangers who could talk openly and compassionately about the issues they were facing. The food that neighbours and friends often bring to the house after the birth of a baby is a valued form of support of a more practical kind. Bed-bound with morning-sickness in my second pregnancy, I was profoundly grateful to the friends who came round to play with my two-year-old for a couple of hours on Sunday mornings, so that my husband could have a bit of respite himself.

Another reason why my friend Ruth found having two children much easier than she'd expected was because she had much better support second time round. 'James didn't want to have children before Hannah was born, and made it clear that if I decided to go ahead, I shouldn't count on him for help. I didn't have many close friends around at that time either – I'd been working in London right up until I had Hannah and commuting from the small village where we actually lived – so I didn't have anyone to turn to, or talk to, or walk to the swings with. It's been completely different with Rachel. I've made good friends in the village, and because I didn't go back to work, I'm more involved in village life generally. James has been more supportive, too. After Rachel was born, Hannah wanted him not me, so he had to help more!'

Having people to take the children off your hands for a bit; having people to help with the physical chores of parenting; having people to lend you a pint of milk when the baby's screaming for a bottle and the three-year-old's fast asleep; having people to make you laugh and remind you that you are a person as well as a parent – this is the kind of support that makes a difference.

Another factor that affects the impact of a second child on you and your family is timing. Often, of course, the matter will be outside your control: you may get pregnant sooner than you intended, or it may take much longer to conceive your second child than you'd wanted. With women now having children later in life, the timing of a second child often ends up having more to do with fertility than planning. Alex lives in Kent and, until two years ago, worked in London as a secretary in a law firm. She had her first child when she was 35. She and her husband Greg planned to have their children close together, 'But it just didn't happen that way. It took five years to conceive the second time, by which time I was 40. My employers weren't very supportive and I hated seeing so little of the children. After a great deal of soul-searching, I decided to stop work altogether. I may go back when they're a bit older but for the moment I'm a housewife.'

Sometimes there will be a conflict of interests about the timing of a second child. Laura, 32, had a traumatic labour with her first child, and in the months following the birth suffered from depression and anxiety attacks. She and her husband, David, an academic, were living abroad at the time, a long way from friends and family, and for Laura, bringing up her first child in a strange country was alienating and stressful. 'I had terrible trouble with breast-feeding. My nipples cracked and bled, and I didn't seem to have enough milk. I couldn't get the baby to latch on properly. The midwives advised me to switch to formula, but it didn't help, because Sam refused the bottle. He was getting more and more distressed and I was getting more and more frantic. The midwives were all different nationalities, some of them barely spoke English, and they all gave conflicting advice about what to do. Different kinds of teats, different kinds of formula, different ways of expressing. It was just awful. And all the time I felt I was starving my own child.' Although Laura was keen to have a second child in theory, she did not feel 'ready' to go through the experience again until her first child was almost five. 'I was very torn between what was best for the children and what was best for me. David wanted to get on with having another child too. In the end, I just had to wait until I felt ready.'

For most of the women I interviewed the age gap between their children seemed to play an important part in their experience of mothering two. Those with the largest age gap between their children, such as Laura, were among the most positive. They had less exposure to the 'two under five' phase that is recognised as so stressful. Because their older child was already in regular daycare, they limited the time spent coping with 'double demands'. In effect, they were having each child one at a time. However, as Judy Dunn says in *From One Child To Two*, there is no magic formula for the timing of siblings. 'There is no "right" or "wrong" interval. Every pattern of timing has its own advantages and disadvantages.'[4]

A smaller age gap will increase the chances of your children being friends, but it will also increase the physical and emotional strain on parents in the first few years. Ultimately, there is no such thing as an 'ideal' age gap. From the child's perspective, an age gap of three years or more is preferable. By this age, your older child will have enjoyed plenty of one-to-one attention from you, will have begun to develop a social world outside the home, and will also be more able to articulate feelings of distress and jealousy. All of these factors make it easier for a child of three or more to cope with the sudden appearance of a rival for your attention and affection. What works best for you will depend on your own personal priorities, which in turn will be shaped by your age, health, finances, work situation. If you want to increase your family size without increasing the strain on you and your partner, you may want to space your children more widely apart. A bigger age gap is harder for the children to bridge, but makes the early years considerably easier for the parents. If your priority is minimising the wear and tear on your self-esteem, your marriage and your furniture, the ideal gap is probably about eighteen years. On the other hand, if you want to get all the stress out of the way as quickly as possible, the smaller the gap the better. As one father of twins told me, 'the ideal gap is exactly eight minutes'.

Whether the balance tips in favour of 'easier' or 'harder' for you personally will depend on which things are easier and which are harder. Life with small children is highly volatile and changes in unexpected ways. A marriage may be weaker than it was first time round, but you may have more money and better childcare. You may have moved house and now be in a nicer area, but be further from family and close friends. You and your partner may have split up, but the lack of marital conflict may make

The Truth About Age Gap

There are a number of myths about age gap, which should not be allowed to influence your decision-making. To set the record straight:

- Intellectual development is not affected by age gap.
- Physical and psychological health are not affected by age gap.
- Birth order and age gap between siblings do not have a significant impact on personality.

A small age gap is no firm guarantee of a good sibling relationship. Other factors are:

- The father's relationship with the older child.
- The relationship between the parents.
- One child feeling less loved, unloved or unfairly treated by parents.
- The compatibility of the children's personalities.

How Was It For You?

Some of the factors that can complicate the transition from one child to two are:

- Having a demanding second child after an undemanding first child.
- Older child adjusting badly to new baby.
- Insufficient support from partner, friends, relations.
- Insufficient support with housework and childcare.
- Previous life events: bereavement, divorce, relationship with own parents and siblings.
- Health problems – physical and mental.
- Money worries.
- Other stress factors: moving house, changing job, bereavement.

it easier to cope with the physical and emotional demands of your children. You may have changed job, and this may have brought wanted or unwanted changes. Then there is the baby itself: is your second child a good feeder, a bad sleeper, the same sex or the opposite sex, peaceful, restless, smiley, colicky? Sometimes events outside the home tip the balance, such as an unexpected redundancy, a bereavement or financial problems. The combination of any of these factors in your life forms the framework for your experience of mothering two children. Some are within your control, others are not. Some are fixed, others are flexible. For some people it will indeed be 'much easier second time round'; for others the experience will be more complicated.

Understanding why you may be a 'low risk' or 'high risk' mother-of-two is not a guarantee of a 'good' experience, anymore than reading up about labour will guarantee a hitch-free birth, but giving some thought to the matter in advance will mean you are as prepared as it is possible to be, and better placed to seek the kind of support or advice you need.

Could the transition from one child to two be made easier? Could the stress and strain that parents and children experience at this critical time of family adjustment be minimised? Could mothers – and fathers – be better prepared for what they're getting into when they decide to have a second child?

Rachel Oliver is a health visitor in Oxfordshire and has run a number of courses for parents expecting a second child. She thinks that preparing parents for life with two children is almost impossible. 'Most people just can't imagine what it is going to be like; it doesn't make much difference telling them in advance because it just doesn't sink in.' Rachel wonders if this is a protective instinct in mothers. 'Parents only really want to focus on the very next step. They can't think beyond the immediate reaction to the baby, and when that goes well, it is a huge relief. We found it more helpful to respond to problems as they actually arose, rather than try to anticipate them.' Shona Gore of the National Childbirth Trust is more optimistic. She has run courses for second-time parents for the last 12 years and seen a huge rise in the number of parents who attend 'refresher classes' before having their second child. 'These classes are becoming increasingly popular, partly because parents can't get the information anywhere else, and partly because the needs of second-time parents are very different from the needs of first-time parents. Second-time mothers know about labour, obviously, but may want to do things differently second time round. They need updating on medical information. They also want to know how to prepare their first-born for the arrival of a sibling.' Shona agrees with Rachel that some aspects of second-time parenthood are best tackled as they arise, rather than in advance, but thinks the solution is to ongoing support *before and after* the baby is born.

Research backs this up. Studies of first-time parents found clear evidence that attending support groups helps people to manage the stresses and strains of the transition to parenthood. Parents who attend weekly groups for the first three months of their baby's life cope better for up to *three years*.[5] One of the few in-depth studies of *second-time* parents also shows that attending antenatal preparation classes is helpful. Couples who had taken part in parenting classes before the birth of their second child were compared with couples who had not had any kind of formal preparation. All the mothers and fathers who'd taken part in classes were coping better in the first month after their second child's birth than the parents who had not been to any classes. The benefits of preparation classes wore off pretty fast however. Four months after their second child's birth, the couples who'd been to classes were coping no better than the ones who hadn't. This doesn't mean to say the classes were worthless. It means that the issues change, and that adjusting to life with two children is a gradual process that takes time and alters over time. Attending parenting classes had helped parents cope with the situations they encountered at the time of their second child's birth, but were not much help when it came to the issues they were running into three or four months later.

Courses preparing parents for the impact of their second child could make a real difference to how parents adjust, but to be really helpful, classes need to be ongoing, and spread throughout the first year – at least – of the second child's life. They need to focus on the key points in the transition period: birth, four months, eight months and a year – and they need to aim at giving parents realistic expectations of what each next phase will bring.

Inevitably, much learning takes place in the doing. What makes these first few years of raising two children so intensely challenging is that beneath the surface of relentless physical needs – the breast-feeding, the bottom-wiping, the face-washing, the clothes-cleaning, the teeth-brushing, the graze-kissing – there are the vast shifting plates of our emotional connections to one another. As parents we are having to change and adapt to cope with the experience of loving and caring for not one but two children. The first-born child, meanwhile, must not only adjust to being and having a sibling, but must find ways to accommodate the changes that this creates in his or her relationship with his or her parents.

With two children, it is not just our focus that has to change, but often our whole approach to bringing up children, to being a parent. In psychoanalytic terms, it may be that the second child creates powerful opportunities for development and growth beyond the fantasies that a first child can embody, but as many mothers-of-two know only too well, it is as easy to be swamped by that day-to-day caring as enriched by it, particularly in the first year or two. The first-born is not the only person in the family reacting and adjusting to the arrival of a second child. We, too, are reacting and adjusting, making changes to the way we mother, and to the way we think of ourselves as mothers. Making the transition from one child to two is a process that takes time and trust and patience. It is the demanding, frustrating, rewarding, fascinating business of loving and caring for our children, day after day after day, that makes this process of change actually happen. Any thinking and preparing we manage to do beforehand can only help to make this process go more smoothly.

'Chase me Mummy!'

Two

LET'S GET PHYSICAL

Until the beginning of the 20th century, having more than one child was both an inevitable outcome of sex and the best insurance policy against genetic extinction. It was not unusual for a woman to be continuously pregnant throughout her married life, but many children never even made it to their first birthday. Two hundred years ago only a quarter of all babies survived their first year of life. As recently as 1872 an enquiry in one area of England found that almost 50 per cent of children died before they were five. Most families would have endured the death of at least one child. Even royalty were not immune: Queen Anne of England bore 17 children, 16 of whom were stillborn or died in infancy, while the longest-living died at the age of 11. Perhaps it was with good reason that the American heiress Consuelo Vanderbilt, who became the ninth Duchess of Marlborough when she married a cousin of Winston Churchill, referred to her two little boys as 'the heir and the spare'.

If there was a high risk of children dying, there was also a high risk of the mother going with them. Until the 1930s, getting pregnant was still one of the most dangerous things a woman could do. In many countries in the world, it still is. Most of us know women whose experiences of pregnancy and childbirth would have killed them a century ago. Of the various medical conditions that made my second pregnancy a misery, at least three of them would have finished me off a hundred years earlier. My only consolation for this thought is that I would have been in excellent company: in 1855 Charlotte Brontë died of *hyperemesis gravidarum* (an acute form of morning sickness) long before the invention of intravenous drips. Nearly 60 years earlier, in 1797, with limited knowledge of medical hygiene, and blood transfusions and anaesthetics not yet in existence, Mary Wollstonecraft had little protection against the blood infection that resulted from a retained placenta and post-partum haemorrhage. She died a few days after giving birth to her daughter, Mary, who later become famous for marrying the poet Shelley and writing *Frankenstein*, a novel about the dangers of creation, aptly enough. Both these women, and many thousands more, died of conditions that continued to be lethal well into the 20th century. The novelist Jane Austen avoided the perils of pregnancy and labour by never marrying, but three of her brothers lost wives in childbirth. On hearing that one of her nieces was pregnant again, she wrote: 'Poor Animal, she will be worn out before she is 30.'

These days we worry about the degree of pain and the best positions for delivery rather than our chances of surviving the ordeal at all. Few women are 'worn out' by pregnancy any more, and from a medical point of view, pregnant women are only of interest if they represent some kind of abnormality.

Yet the individual experience of pregnancy and birth is not so easily reduced. Now that we are likely to bear only a very small number of children, each pregnancy and labour takes on a large significance in our lives. At the same time, giving birth remains one of the most frightening and most dangerous things a woman does in her lifetime (as a rather tactless junior obstetrician chose to remind me the night before my second child was due to be induced). Few of us know anyone who has actually died in labour, but nearly all of us know someone for whom it was a close-run thing, for whom the experience was deeply traumatic, even though they and the baby survived to tell the tale. Giving birth is still a big deal, not just physically, but also emotionally and psychologically. Instead of recognising the enormity of the undertaking, though, we seem to do the very opposite: we are encouraged, and encourage ourselves, to treat this momentous event in our lives as if it were nothing, to shrug it off as if it were the easiest thing in the world, to make out that it affects us only in minor, temporary, positive ways.

The only 'confinement' most of us get these days is confining the tougher aspects of pregnancy and labour to our own homes. Woe betide any woman who drops even the faintest hint that she is finding the creation of a human being an arduous undertaking. Any such complaints, instead of being seen as the natural toll of bearing children, will be taken as an indication of the unnaturalness (even the uselessness) of the mother. From the moment we conceive our first child, we put great effort into keeping up with the boys: not allowing ourselves to drop behind at work, at home, at the gym. Susan Maushart writes in *The Mask of Motherhood*: 'Childbirth has become not only an athletic event, but also an aesthetic one, an arena for personal expression, an opportunity to sculpt transcendence from a fleshly medium of blood and bone and muscle.'[1] It is not, note, a potentially life-threatening lottery in which 'success' depends largely on good luck.

Ironically, while so much apparent attention is given to becoming and being a mother, many core aspects of both these states remains extraordinarily hidden. Why, for instance, is there a custom not to tell even our closest relations that we are pregnant until after the 12th week, on the grounds that that is when the risk of miscarriage drops? If they do miscarry, most women will be more, not less in need of support. (A recent report found that fathers-to-be are even more distressed by miscarriage than their partners.) Why do we try not to tell our employers we are pregnant until months five or six of the pregnancy when we can no longer hide the fact; it is during months two, three and four that we most need their sympathy and tolerance? Why do we congratulate women on leaving hospital the same day as they've given birth, when even after the easiest of labours what they need is rest and respite from the domestic responsibilities that await them back home? Nowadays, as Susan Maushart puts it, 'we are expected to take pregnancy like a man'. This machismo is misplaced and unhelpful during a woman's first pregnancy and labour, and still more so during her second, when she has even more need of support, acceptance and tolerance, even more need of permission to be, quite simply, female.

We don't want to be seen as invalids, of course, but pregnancy is a special state that needs and merits recognition and attention. The effects of pregnancy and labour can be debilitating and long-term. Even when things go smoothly, we still need a bit of time to recover, physically and emotionally.

Pregnancy Second Time Round

From a purely technical perspective, pregnancy and childbirth are usually less dramatic second time round. The medical risks go down and, unless there are known complications, everyone has a better idea of what's in store. But that's all they have: a better idea. In practice, a woman's subjective experience of her second pregnancy and labour is often very different from her first. Second time round, for instance, pregnancy *feels* different. The body has been altered by its prior experience of accommodating a growing foetus and of giving birth, and if you didn't realise this after having your first child, you know about it soon after getting pregnant with your second. The walls of the uterus are thinner and your stomach muscles are slacker after a first pregnancy, so many women find they get bigger quicker, carry lower, and feel the baby moving around inside the womb sooner and more often. You are likely to hear the baby's heartbeat earlier, too – in month four, not five.

Many women find the third trimester more uncomfortable and tiring than they did with their first pregnancy. The growing baby and its increasingly vigorous kicks make more impact both on your silhouette and on your sleep second time round. You may have to endure more of the minor side-effects of pregnancy, such as backache, cramps and indigestion. In a first pregnancy, the hormonal changes have more impact, because your body is being flooded with stuff it has never encountered before; in a second pregnancy, it is the structural changes of child-bearing that are often harder. Your joints have been loosened up by carrying your first child plus heavy baggage: placenta, blood, amniotic fluid and so on and they now hold you together less well, making an assortment of aches and pains more common in second pregnancies.

Most women feel very much more tired throughout their second pregnancy, usually for the simple reason that it is very much harder to find time to rest and relax, to exercise and to eat well. Life is already speeded up by the presence of one child, and during your second pregnancy, your first child's energy levels continue to grow in line with your bump. By the time you reach that stage of pregnancy when your bump is keeping you awake all night with its invisible acrobatics, and your first child is keeping you on the go all day, you may be beginning to wonder whether you were foolish or just totally insane to have wanted another child. The less-than-glamorous truth is that we are less fit, less strong and, of course, less young than we were when we had our first child.

Time itself seems to move at a different pace in a second pregnancy. For some women, it can go intolerably slowly without the excitement, wonder and apprehension to carry you through. But many women say the nine months go much faster in a second pregnancy because they are already so busy with their first child and very often working as well. There's much less time to dwell on what's happening inside them. 'With my first pregnancy, every minute was precious and special,' recalls 34-year-old Fiona, mother of Phoebe and Luke. 'I was conscious of every tiny change in the way I felt or looked, and was forever looking in the books to see just what was happening to the baby at every stage. When I was pregnant with my second child, there wasn't the magic of the first time. Whole weeks went past without my giving it any thought at all. The nine months went much quicker, which was a great relief.'

Laura, mother of seven-year-old Sam and two-year-old Zak, had the opposite experience. She had not enjoyed her first pregnancy and had suffered badly from nausea, backache and heartburn. 'Everyone was blooming except me!' she recalls. 'Second time round I felt less of a misfit, because everyone I knew was finding it hard going, something to endure rather than enjoy.' In some respects, Laura felt she had a better time with her second pregnancy than many of her friends. 'I put off getting pregnant again until Sam was five, so he was at school during the week and I had more chance to rest than friends who were chasing round after their two-year-olds all day. I was so grateful for the time to sit down each afternoon and have a sleep, or maybe go for a swim.'

It is more difficult to find time or energy for regular exercise in a second pregnancy. Late into my first pregnancy I reduced the entire antenatal class to guffaws of laughter by asking the midwife how long one could carry on playing tennis; throughout my second pregnancy, I felt so exhausted that the only kind of exercise that interested me was crawling into bed and going to sleep. Nevertheless, antenatal exercise *is* important. Exercises designed to strengthen and relax the body for pregnancy and labour, as well as a general level of activity in daily life are all as beneficial in a second pregnancy as they were in the first.

The many minor, but still unpleasant, symptoms of pregnancy, such as fluid retention, constipation, flatulence, bleeding gums, nose bleeds, skin complaints, sweating, vaginal discharge, insomnia, incontinence and dizziness tend to recur in each pregnancy, and if you got them before, they will probably be as bad or worse this time round. Heartburn, backache and anaemia are more common in second pregnancies, as are varicose veins in the legs and haemorrhoids. Morning sickness is also more common second time round – probably because women have less time to take care of themselves. But, as with everything to do with babies, one bout of morning sickness does not automatically predict another.

Thirty-eight-year-old Maureen works in PR and is married to Robert, a publisher. They have two children, Kathleen and Ellen. Maureen was very sick throughout her first pregnancy and twice had to spend time in hospital because she became so dehydrated from constant vomiting. She was understandably anxious about what another pregnancy would hold in store. 'None of the doctors could tell me what my chances of another bad pregnancy were, but I was braced for the worst. My husband was dreading it after what we'd been through the last time. He'd had to take time off work, and I was just like an invalid for months. Kathleen was nearly four and a half before I finally plucked up courage to get pregnant with Ellen. It wouldn't have been disastrous if I'd been ill again because Kathleen was at nursery full-time by then, and I could have rested during the day if necessary. But in fact, it was fine. I didn't feel great, but I wasn't sick at all. It was a completely different experience.'

If you suffered during your first pregnancy from pre-eclampsia or hypertension – both conditions that carry serious health risks – you have an increased risk of getting the same conditions second time round. If, on the other hand, you did not have these conditions in your first pregnancy, you are even less likely to suffer them in your second. More good news is that some side-effects of pregnancy, such as sore swollen breasts, may be less pronounced this time round. (There is no ruling on this: some women say they knew they were pregnant far sooner second time because their breasts swelled up within days of conceiving, or because they went off coffee long before they bought a pregnancy tester kit. It's hard to say whether these symptoms actually were more pronounced, or whether the women themselves just knew exactly what those symptoms meant.) If you were horrified to find that your feet had grown after your first pregnancy, stop worrying – they're unlikely to get any bigger this time. And, as long as you don't gain too much weight, you are unlikely at the end of your second pregnancy to have any new stretch-marks to add to your original collection.

We are obviously older when we have our second child than when we had our first, but if you are older than 36, pregnancy comes with a few extra risks attached. Conceiving at all can be more difficult second time round, particularly if you are nearer to your 40th birthday than your 30th. One in eight couples are thought to have trouble conceiving, and even an average, fertile couple stand only a 15 per cent chance of conceiving each month. Once a woman reaches 40, she has a one-in-four chance of being sub-fertile, so if you're over 36 and it takes longer than six months to conceive your second child, you may want to have your fertility checked in case there are any problems.

The risk of a miscarriage is slightly raised by the mother's age, but one or two miscarriages do not mean you won't eventually conceive again or increase the odds of a third miscarriage. For older women embarking on a second child, however, the sense of time urgency can make a miscarriage particularly upsetting. Older mothers also run a greater risk of the baby having some kind of chromosomal abnormality. The risk of Downs Syndrome, for example, is only one in several thousand for a woman in her 20s, one in 110 for a woman of 40, and one in 30 for a woman of 45. More women having a second baby will, therefore, have to decide whether or not to have an amniocentesis, still one of the most accurate ways of finding out if a baby has a genetic defect, and usually routinely offered to women over 37. Amniocentesis can cause a very small number of babies – 0.5 per cent – to miscarry. If this is going to be your last child, or if it has taken a long time to conceive, that risk may still seem very high, and having to decide whether or not to go ahead with an amniocentesis can be very stressful indeed. It may help to discuss not just the procedure, but the risks and implications of your baby having a genetic defect with a trained genetic counsellor. Your GP, midwife or gynaecologist will be able to arrange a referral.

As far as sympathy and support goes, whatever your age, you should steel yourself for something altogether less exalted this time round. The fact is, no one but you cares how often or for how long the baby kicked you in the night; no one but you is interested in watching your stomach ripple and flex with in-vitro antics; no one but you (and possibly your mum) really cares how the second labour went, how much the baby weighs, whether it has hair, or how the breast-feeding is going. Even though you may be even more in need of support and sympathy than first time round, the general attitude from friends and loved ones is usually: 'Been there. Done it.' As American author and mother-of-four Vicki Iovine puts it: 'Unless you are growing sextuplets or kittens in there, you just aren't all that compelling any more.'[2] Even the father-to-be may show rather less interest in you and his second child than you'd ideally like (unless, of course, it is *his* first child). If your partner wouldn't prepare for the first baby, you've no hope of getting him to prepare for the second. If you *were* lucky enough to have an involved partner first time round, don't expect anything of the kind this time round. 'The bottom line is this,' says

Iovine, 'a woman gets "Precious Vessel" status once with each partner, so either suck it up or get yourself a new partner.'[3]

One of the biggest differences between this and your first pregnancy is that this time round you already have a child to look after. One of the biggest differences, from that child's point of view, is that he or she is slowly but surely undergoing a process of displacement from the centre of the universe. This is hard enough for you and your partner to grasp before the baby actually arrives, and it is even harder for your first-born to take on board. When I look at my two children now, I feel confident that the experience of becoming a sibling has been an enriching one for my daughter, but there have been times when I've had my doubts. She has had to make space for her younger brother, she has had to learn to share her physical environment with him, and also, of course, her possessions and her parents. She has had to learn to accommodate his personality, to tolerate his needs, and to accept that sometimes (often, as it seems to us; invariably, as it seems to her) his needs come before her own. I know, because she has told me, that there have been times in the last three years when she would have gladly sent him back to wherever he sprang from. But increasingly, as he advances into his fourth year of life, she is discovering in him a playmate, a companion, an ally, an accomplice. They have great romping games together, riotous hiding games, noisy jumping and chasing games. He can be quite useful at times, fetching and carrying for her. And he can be interesting and funny, too: he makes her laugh. Increasingly, I hear the wonderful words: 'Come on. Let's go and…'

Preparing your first-born for the arrival of a sibling is an important and of course unprecedented aspect of second pregnancy. There is clear evidence that families who do take time to prepare the older child, benefit from doing so. It's not just the children who benefit; the parents do too. A study of 41 American couples, all of whom had attended a course on preparing their first child for the arrival of their second, found that they coped better with *both* children in the first month after the baby's birth than couples in a parallel study who had not attended any kind of preparation class.[4] In particular, the 'prepared' couples found the behaviour of their older child easier to handle and more acceptable. The researchers were not sure if this was because the first child of a 'prepared' couple found the arrival of a sibling less traumatic, or if the parents simply had more realistic expectations of the child. The answer, in all likelihood, is *both*.

Preparing your first child for the arrival of a sibling gives your first-born at least an inkling of the huge change in store, and it gives you, too, a chance to think about these changes from your child's point of view as well as your own.

Janice recalls how she and her husband prepared their son, Gareth, for the birth of their second child. 'I read him stories and talked about what was in my tummy, and towards the end I showed him some photographs of babies curled up in the womb, which he found absolutely fascinating. Jonathan also took over putting him to bed in the last month. I think the preparation helped him cope with Eva once she actually arrived home, but he still acted up a bit with us for a few weeks – waking in the night, having more tantrums than usual, that kind of thing. It was quite hard getting the right balance between turning a blind eye and being firm about certain kinds of behaviour. By about six or seven weeks he seemed to have settled down again.'

However young your first-born, and however relaxed or daunted you feel about turning them into a sibling, it is vital that your child knows that another baby is going to be born *before* the baby actually is born. A child of even 18 months understands and notices far more than we may think, and the unannounced arrival of a new baby would be a terrible shock. If you have been the main carer with your first child, try to get other adults more involved in looking after your first-born before the new baby arrives. Bathtime and bedtime, in particular, are very stressful in the first few weeks if you are the one that both children want. If some of the daily routines can be handed over to another adult in advance of the second baby's birth, your first-born won't feel so excluded and resentful once the innocent usurper appears on the scene. For the same reason, you might want to accustom your older child to short separations from you before the baby is born, particularly if they have never been apart from you. Even the short absence when you are having the baby can be very upsetting for a first-born child if it is the first time she has ever been apart from you. Again, telling your older child what is going to happen before it happens will help her to cope in the event.

Foster your child's curiosity about the new baby in as many ways as possible. Let him help you sort the Babygros into different sizes, or make up the baby's crib. Show him pictures of himself as a baby, look at picture books together about babies, tell him what happened when he was born – all of this will help him formulate some idea of what to expect. Children adore seeing pictures of themselves as babies, and hearing stories about themselves. Many children will also be intrigued by photographs of embryos growing inside the womb, fascinated by the idea that they were once inside you too. There is now quite a wide selection of children's books available – fact and fiction – dealing with the arrival of a new baby in the family. Some of these are straightforward factual accounts aimed at younger children, others look at the jealousy and distress that a new baby can evoke in the first-born. There are some excellent books on the market, but pick your book with care to avoid stories that might suggest problems before they actually arise.

Preparing Your First-born Prior to the Birth

- Talk about the baby: what it's doing in there; what it can see and hear.
- Look at photos together of when your first-born was a baby; talk about what happened when she or he was born – the nice bits!
- Look at books about babies.
- Explain to your first-born what will happen to them when you have the baby. If a home birth, where will they be? If a hospital birth, who will look after them while you're away?
- Talk about how it will be when the baby arrives home. Explain that babies cry!
- Foster your first-born's curiosity about the new baby. Get them to help get the baby's clothes and cot ready.
- Read stories about becoming a sibling with your first-born. Attend to questions about the new baby, and be sensitive to anxieties.
- Get your partner involved. Encourage him to spend time alone with your first child. Their relationship will be your safety net once the new baby arrives, and will make it easier for your first-born to tolerate your preoccupation with the baby.
- Hand over some of the routine childcare tasks to your partner before the baby is born, such as putting your older child to bed, dressing them in the morning.

Labour Second Time Round

A quite astonishing number of women confess to not preparing at all for their second labour. In our first pregnancy, we pack our bag weeks in advance, carefully tick items off against a neatly typed checklist, lovingly fold and refold the tiny Babygros, assiduously store up coins for the payphone. Second time round it's week 39 and we haven't got a checklist, the Babygros are still somewhere in the attic and we've spent all our change on Noddy's car at the supermarket. This cavalier approach borders on lunacy when you stop to consider that second labours are more likely to start on time, and are often much quicker. 'I didn't go to any classes second time round, and I didn't read any books,' recalls my friend Ruth. 'I don't really know why, I just thought I knew all there was to know. As soon as I went into labour with Rachel, I realised I couldn't remember anything! Even though the labour was very straightforward, I really hated it. I didn't feel in control of what was happening.' Giving birth is not like riding a bicycle, something you learn once and never need to learn again; it is more like climbing Everest: it needs thoughtful preparation no matter how often you've done it before. Ideally, this preparation should be spread over several months, and always it should be done with the awareness that something unexpected might happen at any moment.

Your partner, too, may need informing – or reminding – of the differences between first and second pregnancies. When Fiona went into labour with her second child, her husband Peter's main memory from the previous time was of lots of hanging round with nothing much happening. To help the hours pass more swiftly during this labour, Peter took the precaution of popping a book in the hospital bag. The book in question was *War and Peace*, and Fiona was not amused. In the event the baby was born in two hours flat and they didn't have time to unzip the hospital bag, never mind get anything out of it.

The best news about second labours is that, as Fiona and Ruth found, they are usually not only more punctual and speedy, they also tend to be more straightforward and less likely to require medical intervention. Second-time mothers in general are less at risk of complications than first-time mothers, especially if their first labour was straightforward. The baby is more likely to be correctly positioned in second labours, and the labour is also more likely to start spontaneously (rather than needing to be induced). This in turn cuts the chances of needing an epidural by about half (66 per cent of induced labours used epidurals, compared to 36 per cent of spontaneous labours). Second-time mothers also have a much higher chance of a first stage of under six hours, compared to first-time mothers. Having a short first stage in turn increases your chances of having a short second stage. Epidemiologists at the University of Birmingham found, from a study of 11,000 women, that 91 per cent of short first stages (under two hours) were followed by short second stages (under one hour). Of the first-time mothers, 55 per cent had a second stage of at least an hour, compared to only 14 per cent of women who'd given birth before. Compared to women who'd been through a previous labour, first-timers were *four times* as likely to have a second stage lasting an hour or more. Since having a long labour increases your chances of needing an episiotomy, this too is less of a risk in your second labour. The risk of tearing and needing stitches, however, is only slightly reduced in second labours. Two-thirds of women in Britain need some stitching after giving birth, and in the Birmingham survey, only 18.7 per cent of women who gave birth vaginally emerged with intact perineums.[5] Older women, however, run a higher risk of bearing heavier babies, which increases the risk of having a long second stage and needing an epidural, an episiotomy or a Caesarean delivery.

Many women say they feel more in control during the second labour, and that they are more aware of what is happening to them. This combination of control and understanding in turn makes the pain of childbirth seem more manageable. Throughout my second labour, I alternated between, on the one hand, cursing myself for having forgotten how hideously ghastly giving birth is and wondering how I could ever have been so stupid as to do it twice, and on the other hand, fortifying myself with the knowledge that this kind of pain meant the cervix was doing its stuff, and this kind of pain meant I was probably in transition, and this kind of THAT'S-ENOUGH-GET-ME-OUT-OF-HERE-NOW! pain meant the baby was about to be born. Understanding what was going on didn't stop the pain, but it helped me to endure it.

Laura's first pregnancy had ended in a long, difficult delivery, with an epidural, episiotomy and forceps delivery. In complete contrast, she gave birth to her second child at home without the need for any medical intervention other than entynox (gas and air). 'The labour was still quite slow, and still extremely painful, but I felt in control the whole time. We had a wonderful midwife – very sensitive and experienced. It was the labour I'd hoped for. It was wonderful, really. It was as if we'd been given a chance to get it right.'

Not all women will have an easier second labour. Caroline, 39, is a social worker in Leeds. Her husband, Mark, is a scientist, and they have two children, Tom, five, and Bridget, three. Caroline, like Laura, had a long and difficult first labour. The labour was induced and the first stage contractions were very painful. Caroline eventually needed an epidural to manage the pain. As soon as he was born, the baby had to be put straight on to a ventilator as he'd swallowed meconium. On the positive side, the epidural had worked well, she'd had a pain-free second stage and given birth without tearing. 'All in all, it was pretty traumatic,' she recalls, 'and I wasn't looking forward to going through it again.' As Caroline's second pregnancy progressed she felt increasingly anxious about the labour. 'Everyone tells you it'll be fine second time round, but I never really believed them. Especially not once I'd gone past my due date, and knew the baby would probably have to induced, like last time.' Caroline's fears proved well founded. Two years later she still recalls her second labour with evident distress. 'The baby was stuck and nothing was happening. I kept telling the midwife, but she didn't seem to believe me, and I knew something was wrong. I could feel that it wasn't right. In the end, Mark and I were both shouting at her to get a doctor. The doctor took one look at me, and said 'We need to get this baby out'. I had to have a huge episiotomy and a lot of stitches, and the baby was taken straight off to special care because the cord had been wrapped round her neck. The whole thing was ghastly.'

In *Life After Birth*, Kate Figes describes the trauma of her second child's birth and the deep bond it created between her and her partner. 'He was upset by the birth of our second child – seeing me in pain and holding the baby for half an hour after her birth while they tried to stabilise me after heavy blood loss and another Caesarean. But perhaps the most upsetting moment for us both was at the end of the day, when he had to carry our older child away from my bedside after she had held her baby sister for the first time, for she screamed, 'I need my mummy too!' along the hospital corridor, when she realised that I wasn't coming home with them. When he returned to the hospital later that night, he drew the curtain silently around my bed. He put his arms around me and we sobbed uncontrollably together, sobbed for our first-born, sobbed for ourselves and we sobbed with relief. It was a moment of shared intimacy that I will never forget.'[6]

Natalie, a 34-year-old actress, married to David, an accountant, lives in London with her two sons, Benedict, five, and Sebastian, one. Natalie had a particularly complicated first labour, which ended in a failed epidural and a prolonged forceps delivery. She needed two further operations to repair the damage, and was in a fragile state emotionally and physically for many months afterwards. She felt very anxious beforehand about getting pregnant again, and when she discovered in the eighth month of her second pregnancy that the baby was expected to be born weighing 11 or 12 lb, she decided to have an elective Caesarean. 'There was a certain amount of disapproval,' she recalls. 'I think some people felt I was letting the side down. But I didn't want to risk it. I never wanted to go through the horror of that first labour again. I was a bit nervous about having the Caesarean, but it was so calm and relaxed. It felt strange when they were pulling the baby out, but there was no actual pain at all. For the baby, it was a Rolls Royce delivery, so gentle, and I think that's why Sebastian has always been such a relaxed, easy baby. But for me, the recovery period was very hard. I don't regret having a Caesarean because it was infinitely better than another traumatic natural birth would have been, but looking back I think I had a very misguided view of what it would be like. I hadn't understood that it was major surgery, and that as with all major surgery, you feel appalling afterwards. You hurt all over. Every step is painful. Getting into the breast-feeding position is painful. Had I known in advance, I'd still have gone for a Caesarean, but I'd have arranged things differently: no visitors for two weeks; Benedict to my mother for two weeks; full-time round-the-clock help with the baby for at least a month!'

Caesareans, as Natalie discovered, are not the easy option they're often made out to be. They are medically necessary in certain circumstances (for example, if the baby is breech or transverse, if there are triplets, or if the mother has a condition such as *placenta praevia*, pre-eclampsia or active genital herpes), but they do come with risks attached. The number of Caesarean births rises each year. One in eight women in Britain and one in three women in America now gives birth by Caesarean, and alongside this rise is increasing concern in some quarters of the medical profession that the risks have been downplayed too much. The pain that Natalie describes can be excruciating, and it can take many months to subside completely. Around one-third of women who give birth by Caesarean will still not have recovered entirely three months later. As Kate Figes explains in *Life After Birth*, it is very difficult for women to take the recovery time they need after a Caesarean when they are also being encouraged to look after their babies in the same way as other mothers. 'It takes a Herculean effort to heave yourself up on your elbows, twist yourself around and then lift your baby from its cot when it cries,' she writes, 'and that sense of impotence and inability to care properly for one's baby can cause subsequent psychological problems for the mother.'[7] Heavy blood loss also increases the risk of anaemia after a Caesarean, and headaches are another common and unpleasant after-effect.

Whatever form it takes, a difficult first labour invariably leaves a woman with deep fears about what a second labour will be like, and it may not be until you are pregnant for the second time that these anxieties come to the surface. The appeal of a Caesarean for Natalie was that it offered an alternative to the profound ordeal of her first labour, about which she still felt intensely anxious. A cousin of Natalie's, interestingly, had the entirely the opposite experience: her first pregnancy ended with an emergency Caesarean which she found such a traumatic violation that she was determined to have her second child 'naturally', which she duly did three years later. According to Val Harris, a senior midwife at the John Radcliffe Hospital in Oxford, 'Women often find themselves reliving the trauma of their first labour during their second pregnancy and may well need to resolve feelings about the first labour in order to face the second.' Shona Gore, teacher-tutor for the NCT, wholeheartedly agrees. 'Many women bring a great deal of anxiety from their first labour to their second, and a lot of women, and their partners, need a chance to debrief before they give birth again. We've found, though, that second-time parents often feel inhibited about speaking openly about their experience in front of women who have never been through labour. They're much more comfortable talking about their labour experience with other second-time parents.' Gore's experience underlines the value of antenatal classes aimed specifically at second-time parents.

As she also points out, it's not only the labour, but the whole experience of having a first child that sometimes needs going over, particularly if the mother has had a difficult time. 'Women are reluctant to sound too negative in front of first-time mothers, but they may really need to talk about their experiences. I remember one woman bursting into tears with relief at discovering that she was not the only mother who hadn't bonded immediately with her baby.'

Dilys Daws, consultant child psychotherapist at the Tavistock Clinic in London, makes a direct link between a woman's experience of labour and how she manages with a new baby afterwards. 'The anxiety, humiliation and misery of births that are felt to have gone "wrong" can leave a mother too exhausted to make the first steps of getting to know her baby, and mother and baby can find it difficult to learn each other's rhythms. In extreme cases, the mother can feel angry with the baby, as though it is the baby's fault' that she was cheated of the birth she was expecting... All these feelings, if unrelieved, can lead to depression.'[8]

If there are no classes for second-time parents in your area, you may well find that your local midwives run a one-to-one debriefing service of some kind. Many hospitals now offer a counselling service specifically designed to help women debrief after traumatic labours. There is no time limit, and some women will find it is not until many years later that they are able to think and talk about what happened to them. However, it is more usual for women to want to talk over what they've been through fairly soon after the birth itself and, as Val Harris and Shona Gore say, the second pregnancy can be a key time to address and resolve issues and concerns related to your previous experience of labour.

Pregnancy and Labour Second Time Round

Things tend to go more smoothly second time round. Some medical conditions and minor symptoms, however, are more likely with a second child.

MORE RISK OF	LESS RISK OF
Miscarriage	Wrong positioning of placenta or baby
Minor side-effects, e.g. heartburn; backache; anaemia; varicose veins; piles	New stretchmarks
	Hypertension (unless you had it last time, in which case high risk)
Morning sickness	
Chromosomal abnormalities, e.g. Downs syndrome	Pre-eclampsia (unless you had it last time, in whichcase high risk)
	Induction (which also reduces the likelihood of needing an epidural)
Heavier baby (if 36 or over, which also increases risk of needing an episiotomy, stitches or Caesarean)	Long labour
	Long second stage

And After – Second Time Round

Immediately after giving birth, you will probably be in better shape than last time. Emotionally, the experience is usually much easier to process because the profound shock of labour is rarely as intense second time round. Physically, too, you are likely to be in better shape, although migraine-type headaches are more common in the few days after your second child is born, and those painful contractions when the baby latches on to feed can also be worse. In the longer-term, real physical recovery is usually slower. In *The Best Friends' Guide to Surviving the First Year of Motherhood*, Vicki Iovine recalls how she checked out of hospital so soon after the birth of her second baby that 'the doctors had barely cut the umbilical cord'. The reason for such haste? Anxieties about her first-born. With hindsight Iovine thinks this neither necessary nor wise. Her advice to all second-time mothers: 'After delivering your second baby, stay in the hospital as long as they will let you.'[9] For most mothers, this is a rare interlude of rest and calm. This is precious time alone with your new baby.

One of motherhood's great mysteries is how life can be so physically tiring, yet make so little impact on one's shape or weight. Feelings of dismay at the sight of yourself in a full-length mirror, well into the second year of your second child's life, are *absolutely normal*. Skin is slower to tighten up; muscle tone is slower to return; the pelvic floor turns to mush; abdominal muscles take longer to knit together again; breasts take a pasting: mine were a disappointment after one bout of breast-feeding, a complete disaster after two. Weight loss may be slower too. This is partly because when you're looking after two children, there is even less time to take regular exercise. An overwhelming desire to fit into your size ten lycra jeans three months after giving birth to your second child is even more unrealistic than it was three months after giving birth to your first. If it took six months to get back to your previous weight after the first pregnancy, allow a year after your second. The good news is that your feet get bigger only after your first baby, and your breasts may make a minor comeback in three or four years' time.

'Are you doing your pelvic floor exercises?' a friend and mother-of-three asked sternly after the birth of my second child. 'Yes,' I replied, 'well, when I remember.' A year down the line I began to understand why she'd asked, and why in that voice. First time round my pelvic floor sorted itself out; second time it definitely needed some assistance. Before I had children, I often used to wonder why motherhood seemed to render women so unadventurous; two children later, I fully understand the hidden risks of a bouncy castle.

A second bout of pregnancy and childbirth inevitably takes its toll on your body, and it can take much longer to persuade anal/vaginal/perineal/abdominal/pectoral muscles to behave as you'd like them to. Fiona, mother of five-year-old Phoebe and two-year-old Luke, observed wryly, 'My bottom still turns inside out when I go to the loo.' Janice, mother of Gareth and Eva, can't stand the way 'the swimming pool disappears up my insides, and then reappears in the changing rooms'. After your second baby the true purpose of superplus tampons and month-round panty liners becomes apparent.

Remember that sheet of paper that the midwives gave you in hospital just after you'd given birth, and which got turned into a hat for your toddler the first day he came in to meet the new baby? That was the instruction sheet for your pelvic floor exercises. You were supposed to start doing this exercise as soon as possible after the birth, and to continue doing it as often as possible (what, like twice a decade?) once back home in the newly enlarged bosom of your family.

We are told that this is a good exercise to do on the phone, in check-out queues, at bus stops and so on. But the people who tell us this have clearly forgotten (or never known) just what high-stress occasions these are for the mother-of-two, who no longer knows the meaning of the phrase 'standing still'. Your average mother-of-two at a bus stop will be unstoppering the baby's bottle; singing 'Baa Baa Black Sheep'; folding/unfolding the pushchair (one-handed); attempting to locate the second shoe; wondering where her purse is; wondering if she remembered to put any money in it; hauling her pre-schooler out of the path of an oncoming bus; dissuading said pre-schooler from regaling the woman behind with a blow-by-blow account of this morning's marital row – and generally impersonating an octopus on speed. The average mother-of-two at a bus stop is displaying the mental dexterity of an Einstein, the physical endurance of a Houdini, the emotional stoicism of a Gandhi. The average mother-of-two deserves accolades for surviving five minutes at a bus stop, not criticism for failing to exercise her pelvic floor at the same time. Einstein, Houdini and Gandhi *combined* couldn't have exercised their pelvic floors in her situation.

Incontinence is a common side-effect of bearing children, and one that gets more common with each pregnancy. It is also very, very little talked about. Stress incontinence (that is, wetting yourself when you laugh, sneeze, run, jump and so forth) is more likely to affect older women, non-first-time mothers and women who give birth to larger babies. The older you are when you give birth, the more likely it is that problems with incontinence will be chronic and long-term. Incontinence affects around one in four women. After a first labour, around 18 per cent of women will suffer from long-term incontinence; that figure rises to 30–35 per cent after a second labour, and to 40–50 per cent after a third. The *Health After Childbirth* survey found that, of the significant number of women who did have some kind of incontinence, a staggering 78 per cent still had problems after a year, yet very few had mentioned it to their doctors, or sought any kind of treatment.[10]

Pelvic Floor Work-out

Aim to do this exercise five or six times a day, when your bladder is empty. Aim to slowly increase how long you can hold the muscles for, and the number of repeats. If you are still experiencing problems after three months, talk to your GP, who will be able to arrange a referral to a physiotherapist or gynaecologist.

1 Tighten the muscles around the anus, as if stopping a fart. Don't tighten your buttock muscles, or hold your breath.

2 Tighten the muscles around the urethra, as if holding in a wee. Keep breathing.

3 While still holding the front and back pelvic muscles, pull up the muscles in the middle, around the vagina.

4 With the whole pelvic area now tightened, hold for a few seconds, but only for as long as is comfortable, then release in reverse order: middle, front, back.

5 Repeat several times, until muscles feel tired.

Incontinence needn't be a long-term problem, but it gets harder to treat as you get older. In extreme cases, surgery may be needed, but for most women, the annoyance, inconvenience and sheer embarrassment of minor incontinence can be dealt with by following a course of exercises designed to strengthen the muscles of the pelvic floor. Remembering to go to the loo regularly and cutting down on tea and coffee, both diuretics, can also help.

Incontinence is one of the more common problems that afflict women after giving birth, but one of the shocking findings of the survey of 11,000 women in Birmingham was the number of women suffering from a whole host of physical and mental ailments, occurring with much greater frequency than had previously been supposed. Very few of us, it seems, emerge completely unscathed from doing what Mother Nature intended us for. The Birmingham survey made a particularly important contribution to our knowledge about the impact of childbirth because unlike earlier studies it didn't focus only on first-time mothers; almost 40 per cent of the women surveyed had had a second child or more. According to Christine MacArthur, director of the study, 'Our enquiries revealed an enormous and previously unrecognised problem: a level of post-partum morbidity and impaired health far beyond anything which might have been expected.

These women (many of them second-time mothers) suffered a wide range of different symptoms, many of which had become chronic, resulting in a high prevalence of long-term health problems.'[11]

Complacency about the 'naturalness' of pregnancy and childbirth is clearly misplaced when it leaves so many of us battle-scarred in mind and body. With a second child, we are perhaps emotionally more prepared and more resilient, but as the Birmingham study showed, the physical toll on our bodies accumulates with each child. At the same time, the space and opportunity for recovery diminishes.

First of all, you already have a child to look after as well as a newborn baby, and it's therefore much more difficult to take the time you may need to rest and exercise. You may be keen to get back to normal for your older child, but don't expect to be ready for active service the day you get back from hospital. Your older child has waited a long time, but explain that he may have to wait a bit longer still before you can lift him, chase him, and so on. Again, if you can give your child realistic expectations about what it will be like when the baby arrives *before* it arrives, it will be easier for all of you.

Secondly, some GPs, midwives and health visitors assume that second-time mothers need less support because they've 'done it before', whereas in reality every labour is different, and some women need more information and support after they have their second child than they did after their first. If you feel something is wrong, insist on attention, and don't be fobbed off with less than you feel you need. Ask all the questions you want and don't assume that you should know the answers simply because you've had a baby already – you may well be asking totally different questions this time.

Your recovery process may also be slowed down because there is less support from family, friends and partner this time round. Your partner will be taken up with your older child, and not so able to look after you, or help you with the new baby. Friends and neighbours are less likely to bring round food or offer to help with the shopping. Generally less fuss is made either of you or the baby. This means that there may not be so many spare hands to rock the cradle when you desperately need to take a nap or make a cup of tea. Try not to take other people's behaviour as your cue; instead ask for what you feel you need. Enlist friends to take the older one off your hands for an hour or two, or buy a loaf of bread on the way over. Ask grandparents if they can help out for week or so. If there's no one around, and you're really finding it hard to cope, ask your health visitor if there are any drop-in centres or post-natal groups in your area. Sometimes it is just the company of other adults that makes all the difference to how well you feel you are managing. Health visitors can miss milder cases of post-natal depression because mothers often perk up dramatically when they have other people to talk to. As child psychotherapist, Dilys Daws explains: 'Some mothers are only really depressed when alone with the baby; in the company of an interested health visitor they may feel cared for, and not at all depressed – quite a diagnostic problem.'[12]

Things are usually pretty hectic after the birth of a second child, and a combination of children's demands, housework and maternal machismo can lead many women to neglect their health, or ignore symptoms that could be treated, and may need treating. It's not just other people who underestimate our need for time and support: we ourselves don't make sufficient allowance for the physical toll that pregnancy and childbirth take, nor for the fact that we need some recovery time afterwards. In *The Mask of Motherhood* Susan Maushart identifies three aspects of mothering that create problems for women, and in each case, these problems tend to be accentuated, not relieved, by the birth of a second child. The first is the isolation in which we carry out so much mothering of small children; the second is the fact that most mothers are usually in sole charge; even the newest of new men still tends to be in a support role rather than a job share, particularly in the early years of a child's life when the physical demands on the mother are greatest; the third is that few of us have sufficient information and knowledge in advance to prepare us adequately for the practical realities. 'For many women,' writes Maushart, 'the result is a lethal cocktail of loneliness, chronic fatigue and pain.'[13] Our best protection against the downsides of a second pregnancy and labour is not stoicism, but a willingness to drop the façade of invincibility and instead speak openly and honestly about our fears, hopes and needs at this new turning point in our lives. Psychologist Harriet Goldhor Lerner has written that 'pretending is so closely associated with femininity that it is, quite simply, what the culture teaches women to do'.[14] But as Susan Maushart puts it: 'To see motherhood properly... is to see it heroically, which means making full acknowledgment of the pain, the dangers, and the risks and taking the full measure of glory for its exquisite rewards.'[15]

Three

WAYS OF LOVING

There are many ways of loving your children. The first year or two after the birth of your second child is a period of transition for you, your partner and your children. Your own feelings must shift and re-form to enable you to encompass, emotionally and mentally, the realities of two small beings, the ebb and flow of two relationships. But with two children to keep in heart and mind, most mothers find that there is much greater fluctuation in their feelings than when there was only one.

The big, unaskable, unanswerable question in the minds of most mothers who are pregnant with their second child is this: how will I ever be able to love another child as much as I love my first? Even considering *having* a second child can feel like a betrayal of your first-born. To think of yourself actually *loving* another child is, quite simply, unthinkable. 'Oh, don't worry, you will,' people tell you airily. But you still don't quite believe them. Then you have your second child, and you discover, amazingly, that they were right.

Except that it's not always quite that straightforward. Most women find that there is a period of adjustment, a period of weeks or months during which they *gradually* discover how to manage not only caring for, but loving, two children at once. If you're one of the lucky ones, love for your second child comes flooding in without touching your feelings for your first child. Many women, however, find that it takes a while for loving feelings for their new baby to take hold, and that to begin with, responding to the new baby's needs while also trying to attend to an older child is quite a challenge. Some women find it takes them longer to feel connected with their second child; or they find that their feelings for their new child are different from first time round – more tender, less anxious, more protective, less intense. When a second child is the same sex as the first, there can also be an initial feeling of disappointment, of anticlimax. This kind of mismatch between what you think you should be feeling and what your feelings actually are can be very distressing.

Deborah is the mother of two daughters, Zoe and Caitlin, now aged six and four. She works part-time as a physiotherapist and is married to John, an engineer. Deborah went through a long period of feeling very guilty about her feelings towards her second child: 'I didn't feel any great love towards Caitlin for a long time after she was born. I just adored Zoe, my older daughter, more and more. I was very identified and bound up with her, and didn't really know where this new baby was supposed to fit in. I couldn't really handle the baby at all, and it was a long time before I really began to love her. I just wasn't interested in looking after a small baby. I resented her for being so dependent on me. Later on, it changed, and I did fall in love with her. Now she's four and she's adorable. If anything I worry that Zoe misses out a bit because Caitlin and I are so close, but it wasn't like that to begin with at all. It made me very miserable. I remember ringing up my mum one day, and crying down the phone, saying, "I'm so frightened I'll never love Caitlin the way I do Zoe." But almost as soon as I said it, it passed. Now I find it hard to believe I ever felt that way.'

What Deborah is describing is the process of adapting from loving one child to loving two. Like many women, she worried that she was an unnatural mother for failing to fall like a thunderbolt for her new baby. She found it hard to accept that the much slower process that she experienced was also natural. If it were any other context than motherhood, we would simply laugh at the idea of being able, overnight, to change the shape and direction of our devotion, but because we're talking about motherhood we leap to the conclusion that any problems we may be having are our own fault.

Equally natural, though even less mentionable, is that in the first few months of being a mother-of-two, many women find that loving their *first* child is the problem, not loving their second.

Caroline, mother of five-year-old Tom and three-year-old Bridget, says this is what she found hardest in the early months after her second child was born. 'I hadn't thought much about loving the baby before she actually arrived. It was impossible to imagine loving anyone other than Tom, but since everyone said I would love the new baby, I just decided to believe them. Once Bridget was born, the problem was that I *only* wanted to love her. I wanted to gaze and gaze at her all day long, but instead there was this older child wanting my attention the whole time. I found it very hard not to feel irritated with Tom for constantly taking me away from the baby.'

When you try to tell mothers-of-one that they might temporarily experience an alteration, maybe even a tiny diminution, in their affections for their first-born, they look at you with horror and contempt, as if you'd suggested drowning a kitten. I know this because I was one of those mothers. Only a year before my son was born, I'd taken my daughter to our local swimming pool, and while we were changing, I found myself listening with shock and astonishment to the mother in the next cubicle. She had two children in tow, a boy of about four and a baby of about eight months. 'There, my precious! We're going swimming!' she cooed to the baby as she gently fitted him into his swimming trunks. Then she swung round and snarled at the older boy (who was not obviously doing anything wrong): 'Stop that, do you hear! Just stop it this minute!' What a vile woman, I thought. How could she be so foul to her own child? I repeated this story to a friend, a mother of two small boys, a few weeks later. 'Ah, yes!' she said, with the knowing smile of experience on her lips. 'You think you'll never be like that, but your second child comes along and sure enough…' I didn't just *think* I'd never be like that; I *vowed* I'd never be like that. And then my second child came along, and sure enough

For Caroline, this sense of disconnection from her older child lasted for about a year. 'I came home from hospital when the baby was two days old and was very keen to get back to normal as quickly as possible, for Tom's sake. I didn't want him to feel pushed out or excluded, and as a result I probably went too far the other way. I was playing hide and seek under the bed the day after giving birth to Bridget!' At first Caroline's feelings were focused on her older child rather than on the new baby, but over the next few weeks that changed. 'I was very tired and not getting much help from other people, and as the baby got more demanding I found I just wasn't coping with Tom. He seemed so big and clumsy and noisy, and I was often short-tempered with him. Some days I just seemed to be shouting at him the whole time. I'd just be longing for Mark to come home from the office and take him off my hands. I'd be thrusting Tom into his arms before he'd even got through the door!'

Caroline felt anxious and upset about the distance that had grown up between her and her son, and worried that having a second child had caused irreparable damage to their relationship. 'There was this huge sense of loss, but I didn't know what to do about it. I didn't know whether there was anything I could do about it. I felt very ashamed of myself for not feeling more loving towards Tom, but for most of the first year after Bridget was born, Tom and I just didn't get on. We didn't seem to like each other very much. I tried to talk to my husband about it, but he couldn't really understand. In his eyes, Tom was the same lovely little boy he'd always been. Nothing had changed. It caused us both a lot of grief. Mark found it hard to be supportive when he actually felt quite angry with me for not being more loving towards Tom.'

Caroline identifies one aspect in particular of second-time parenthood that can be painful to admit to and hard to handle, namely a disjunction between your feelings for your children and your partner's feelings for them. Fathers often take longer to bond with their younger child than they did with their first, especially if they're very close to and involved with their first-born. A first child is a shared focus, a joint project, a link between you, but when there are two children, parents often cope with the double demands by splitting the responsibility: in most cases, the mother takes the baby while the father takes the older child. Instead of being a link, children can become a wedge, pushing each parent in different directions, not only physically, but emotionally.

Simple lack of exposure to their new child often slows down the bonding process for many men, and from the older child's point of view, this may be highly beneficial, since it ensures they remain the centre of at least one parent's affection. But fathers themselves can feel anxious about their 'lack of feeling' for their second child. 'I don't really feel I know her/him yet,' is the way they put it. Because men tend to be less intensely involved with their second child, particularly in the first few months, they are also less able to be sympathetic and understanding if their partner is struggling with ambivalent feelings for the first-born. Caroline said that her husband, Mark, was *angry* with her for not feeling more loving towards their son. Anger might seem at first glance a surprising reaction, but then is it really surprising that fathers should identify with their older child in this situation? After all, they too may well be experiencing something of an attention-deficit; feeling extra-protective of their first-born may be in part an expression of their own sense of being pushed out by the newcomer.

None of which does much to alleviate the anxiety and stress for the mother of not feeling for a child what she thinks she ought to be feeling. For Caroline, what slowly made the difference was, simply, time. 'It was a very, very gradual process. I remember that around Bridget's second birthday, I was definitely feeling that Tom and I were closer again. Maybe it's as Bridget became that bit less dependent, I don't know, but Tom and I slowly became friends again.'

Once your second child arrives on the scene, your first stops being the baby. From one moment to the next, your first-born undergoes a drastic metamorphosis from sole to shared focus of your attention and love. First-born children never get as much attention again after the birth of a sibling, nor as much physical affection. They often recognise this more clearly than we do. No matter how often you tell a jealous child that you have two arms and two knees, they know they're getting less than before. If you're honest, so do you.

I remember my husband bringing my daughter to the hospital to see me and meet her little brother when he was a day old. She scrambled up on to the bed, her elbows digging into me, her none-too-clean hands all over the baby's tiny face, and before I could stop myself the fateful word had popped out. 'Careful!' The chasm between the delicate, fragile new-born infant and the robust, determined toddler was vast and unbridgeable, and into its depths plunged most of my parenting standards and ideals.

In the coming weeks, however hard I tried not to, I kept hearing myself telling my daughter off. 'Don't!' and 'Stop' and 'Wait' and 'Sshhh!' were forever on my lips. I had become a Jekyll-and-Hyde mother, tender and sweet one moment, cross and impatient the next. It was a heartbreaking business. Yet it was hard *not* to feel irritated when she commandeered all the freshly washed Babygros for her teddies, or climbed into the Moses basket with her mud-caked wellingtons on. It was hard *not* to get annoyed when she clambered on to my shoulders whenever I sat down to breast-feed, or put her face right up against the baby's just when I'd got him to doze off. I was awash with hormones and ragged from lack of sleep; she was ragged and awash too, with something altogether more complicated, but no less overwhelming. But somehow, knowing this didn't help; knowing how confused she was feeling, did not make it any easier to be patient, tolerant or understanding. I'd worried so much about how I should ever love the baby; in fact the terrible truth was that in those early days after the baby was born, it was my daughter I had difficulty in loving. Only late at night, when I'd tiptoe into her room to kiss her goodnight and pause for a moment to watch her sleeping face, lips slightly parted, a wisp of blonde hair curling round a rosy cheek, was I able to feel the steady, unadulterated tenderness of before.

Coping with the way your feelings for your first child can change, and allowing yourself time and space to adapt to the loss of that unique one-to-one bond that often exists between mothers and their first-born, is undoubtedly one of the most hidden and upsetting aspects of second-time motherhood. Loving more than one child at once does not always come easily; the real problem is our expectation that it should.

Adjusting to Loving Two

American psychologist Robert Stewart followed 41 families from a few months before the birth of their second child to a year after, questioning both parents separately and in detail about various aspects of their lives. The researchers also interviewed the older child, carried out family observations, and held parent-group discussions. Almost unprecedented in social research projects, all the families remained in the study until it was completed. One of the findings was that both *levels* of stress and *sources* of stress changed in second-time families. One month after the new baby's birth, for example, mothers were much more stressed by the demands of the newborn, than by the behaviour of their first-born. By the end of the first year, however, the first-born had become the source of far more stress than the second-born.[1]

During the course of the first year after the birth of a second child, the relationship between a mother and her younger child gradually evolves, becoming deeper and more intense as the months pass. At the same time, the relationship between mothers and their first children becomes more strained, as they have to renegotiate the terms of their relationship to make space for the newcomer. Shona Gore of the NCT has seen this happen again and again, but says it is almost impossible to prepare mothers in advance. 'You can't say to people prior to the birth that they may go through a period of falling out of love with their first child, even though it's such a common experience. Instead you try and get them to think about how big their older child's shoes will look, and how demanding their older child will seem compared to a small smiley baby so it's not such a shock when it happens.'

As we've already seen, the model of mothering handed down through popular and professional channels tends to be based on the experience of first-time mothers. This model not only shapes in unhelpful ways our expectations about the practical aspects of life with *two* children. It also shapes our expectations about the emotional experience of mothering two children. Before our second child is born, instead of imagining ourselves loving another child, we imagine ourselves loving our first child *all over again*. Instead of trying to imagine what it might be like loving two different children at the same time, we imagine loving them one at a time. The reality is something that most of us don't even get close to. Instead, we carry on working to a romantic model of two people locked in intense relation to one another. The manuals, the magazines, the self-help books all accept this model of mothering as the norm, all aim at providing mothers with information, guidance and techniques for improving, enriching, managing, as well as just plain surviving, this one-to-one relationship. It is, in a way, a natural progression from the teen-mags and love stories that girls gorge on in adolescence, a maternal version of the same scenario: two people fall in love, they strive to make each other happy, and although there are the inevitable frustrations, misunderstandings and conflicts along the way, but with selflessness, loyalty and devotion they can be overcome.

This romantic ideal has been applied to mothering throughout the Western world, even though most mothers are not in the luxurious position of having only one child to love and care for. For most mothers the dyadic love affair is a relatively brief episode in their maternal lives. Although most of the information and guidance we receive about mothering assumes that a woman will be relating to one child at a time, most mothers will be relating to *more than one* child at a time. When we see a woman snapping at her children in the supermarket, we look away, disapprovingly: she does not conform to the romantic ideal and we do not know where to put her in our mental storehouse. What she does conform to, of course, is the reality of getting round a supermarket with a heavy trolley and two fractious children who are taking it in turns to want to eat something/drink something/get out/hit each other, or even, as my son did on one occasion, lob apples at the other shoppers. Generally speaking, this a stressful experience, not a romantic one. For most mothers, it is also decidedly normal.

'The majority of women who bear one child go on, quite soon afterwards, to bear another,' writes psychologist Penny Munn, 'yet current psychological models of mothering have very little to say about the processes involved in mothering more than one child.'[2] There is something curiously infantile in this bias, as if the psychoanalysts and psychologists of the last 100 years have formulated views of the mother-child relationship based on a child's-eye view, with the focus on the *child's* relationship with the mother, rather than on the whole web of interconnected relationships that exist within the family. Although the reality of mothering as most of us experience it will involve a series of triangular relationships, it is still the romantic 'couple' model of mothering that we aspire to. This in turn leads to the feelings of frustration and failure that so many women go through when they become mothers-of-two or more. We are trying to match ourselves to a model that is entirely the wrong shape and must painfully contort ourselves in the process.

The basic problem, as Munn points out, is that 'a model of mothering based on ideas of romantic love assumes implicitly that a good mother will replicate a nurturing, romantic relationship with each successive child'. The only way to replicate the relationship, of course, is for the mother to replicate herself. If only maternal cloning were that simple! And yet this is what many second-time mothers try to do: we try to have two relationships simultaneously without allowing either to impinge on the other. On the basis of a study of 40 second-time mothers, Munn concludes: 'The metaphor of mother-child love as a romantic attachment is accepted within our culture because it is a familiar, well-tried way of understanding relationships. Adults know what it is like to feel loved, rejected, jealous and so on, and are able to use these experiences to empathise with infant experience. This does not necessarily mean that the metaphor is accurate, or appropriate to the actual experience of the infant.'[3] Or the mother!

To add another layer of complexity to the situation, a growing number of children are now born into households that already contain older offspring by a previous marriage. Sally and Martin have two sons, aged eight months and three; Martin also has three children by his first marriage. Sally feels that the existence of Martin's 'other family', as she calls it, has impacted on the way she has related to her own children in various ways. 'When we had our first child, Dan, I felt Martin was the expert, because he'd already had children and knew everything there was to know, while I was this complete beginner. I'd ask him for advice and defer to him as the experienced parent. Martin has had an incredibly intense bond with Dan since he was born, but for a long time I felt a bit of an outsider. Added to that, Dan is just like Martin, and looks very like Martin's other children. With Jacob, it's quite different. I feel I have more of a right to love him. My feelings for him have a great ease. I understand him and I understand my love for him. Added to that he's more like me, he looks more like me. Martin's older children are very loving towards my two, and in many ways having Jacob and Dan has helped my relationship with them, but I still find it quite a strain when they come for weekends, because as well as looking after my own children, I have to take the older children's needs on board too. In their eyes, I'm always the 'other' woman who stole their dad, and they're very quick to take offence if I say or do something they don't like. Basically, it's bloody hard work, and sometimes I can feel very resentful about Martin giving over his weekend to these other children, rather than concentrating on our two. But of course they are his children too.'

Celia has two children, aged four and one. She is no longer married to the father of her first child, and she and both children live with the father of her second child. She is still in contact with her ex-husband, and they get on well, which makes the practical side of things easier. Emotionally, however, there are less resolvable issues: 'Put it this way: one of my children is the product of a marriage that failed, the other is the outcome of a relationship that is deeply fulfilling. That's bound to have an effect. I think it's hardest for my daughter, because she lives with her stepfather, not her father, whereas my son is with both his parents. I don't know whether they feel that yet, or whether they will feel it later on, but I am very alert to the risk that my daughter might feel marginalised.'

Sometimes, there will be deep-seated reasons why loving two is causing you particular problems. After her second child was born, Tania found that her feelings towards her first child underwent a profound change. 'It was as if a switch had gone in my head. I only wanted to be with Saffron and felt nothing for Megan. I tried to hide it from her, but she could sense the change in my feelings and as time went on she became more and more agitated and demanding and clingy, and I found her more and more annoying and unlovable. It was a horrible experience, for both of us.' When her younger child was a year old, Tania recognised that the problem was not going to go away of its own accord, and that her emotional coldness was causing her older daughter considerable distress. She talked to her GP and was referred to a psychotherapist. Over six sessions, the therapist helped Tania to make links to her own childhood. 'My mother was a very forceful, powerful person, and right from the start with her children it was a case of divide and rule. It was never said explicitly, but she loved me more than my older sister, and we all knew it. My sister was the clever one and I was the loved one. My sister was ambitious, I was kind. It was my mother's way of coping – she doled out attributes and then set about enforcing them. Rather than seeing the good and bad in each of us, she made my sister the bad one and me the good one. Through seeing the therapist, I realised that I was re-enacting all the experiences from my own childhood that I had so hated. Things obviously didn't change overnight, but I have no doubt that seeking help when I did has saved my relationship with Megan, and maybe with both my daughters.'

For the majority of women who experience a change in their feelings of love, the cause will not be deep-rooted unhappiness, but simply the process of adjusting to loving two children rather than one. In this context, age gap *does* seem to make a difference. Women whose children are very close in age, i.e. less than two years, may find it easier to keep in mind the baby-ness of both their children. Celia, 34, is a single mother. Her children, Benjamin and Frances, were born only 14 months apart. 'Frances was still in nappies, still in a cot, still drinking from a bottle, still very much a baby herself. The difficulties I experienced were more to do with the practicalities of coping with two babies simultaneously, because she was still obviously very dependent on me in all sorts of ways, but I didn't feel any less love for her. Almost my first thought after I'd given birth was: "Where's my little girl? I want to see Frances." I don't think my feelings towards her have changed very much. Perhaps I feel a bit more protective towards her, aware that she is having to cope with this big adjustment in her life. But she still seems as sweet and funny and lovable as before.'

Where Did Our Love Go?

Losing a sense of closeness with a child can feel intensely uncomfortable and worrying, but is usually temporary. Emotions aren't turned on like electric lights. They grow and develop and fluctuate. Try to trust that the connection between you and your child is still there and will re-emerge with time once life settles down again.

● Believe that your relationship will recover. If it was close and loving before, there is every reason to trust that it will be close and loving again.

● Get out your first-born's baby album and remind yourself how adorable and agreeable your recalcitrant child can be/once was/might possibly be again.

● Make yourself say and do something affectionate towards the child you're finding hard going, even if you don't feel like it.

● Don't expect to have exactly the same feelings for both your children. Realise that your relationship with each child is unique and that your feelings about each child are bound to be different.

● Make time to chat with your older child about your changed situation, which is confusing for you both. The aim is to acknowledge your child's feelings, not to burden him or her with your anxieties about your own.

● Allow yourself time to bond with your new baby, away from your first-born, but don't expect the relationship to happen overnight.

● Allow yourself time to reforge your relationship with your first child, away from the baby.

● Enlist the help of family and friends, or if necessary buy in help from a babysitter, nanny or childminder, to ensure that you get regular time alone with each child.

● If you still feel unloving to either your first or second child after a year, talk to your GP or health visitor about a referral for specialist help, as there may be more deep-seated reasons for your feelings.

Women with children more than four years apart also seem to find it easier to make emotional space for their younger child without pushing out their older one, often because the older one is already launched into a world beyond the home and forming emotional and social attachments with other children and adults. This obviously takes some of the pressure off the mother, as Laura, mother of seven-year-old Sam and two-year-old Zak, has found. 'I didn't find it difficult to hold loving feelings towards both children at once,' she says, 'but then I wasn't often on my own with them both. Sam was at school by the time Zak was born. He often wants to go and play with other children after school or have friends back to play here. Most of the time when I do have both of them at home, my husband's at home too. I'm sure that makes it a lot easier, because there's usually someone free to respond to each child's needs.'

Laura's experience supports the view of psychotherapist Martha Heineman Pieper and psychiatrist William Pieper, co-authors of *Smart Love*. After working for many years with young children and adolescents, many with serious behavioural difficulties, the Piepers have formulated a philosophy of child-rearing that is as controversial as it is successful. Based on their clinical experience, the Piepers are convinced that all problems in children's behaviour arise out of inner unhappiness. In their view, developmentally inappropriate expectations on the part of the parents are one of the chief causes of this inner unhappiness. (Insisting that a three-year-old has perfect table manners, or that a four- or five-year-old can wipe his or her own bottom are a common age-inappropriate expectation.) The Piepers have found that rigidly or harshly enforcing such expectations without regard for a child's feelings can profoundly undermine a child's development. Sharing is another key area in which parents tend to have hugely unrealistic expectations of their children, and this extends to sharing parents.

According to the Piepers, we would serve the interests of all our children much better if we left at least a three-year age gap between them. 'Children under the age of three still need a lot of your focused attention if they are to develop an unshakeable primary happiness.'[4] When mothers of very young children say they feel torn between the needs of their baby and their toddler, they are not incompetent, or unnatural, they are *in tune*. They are showing their sensitivity to the conflicting interests of their children. Babies and toddlers both want and need uninterrupted, focused care-giving. They are not easily able to tolerate your emotional distraction or dividedness. A sensitive mother will often find it hard to love two small children simultaneously, because in responding wholeheartedly to the emotional needs of one, she inevitably ends up neglecting the emotional needs of the other.

All of the women I interviewed who'd had their second child before their first was three years old, experienced some conflicting feelings about loving their children; in every case, this internal conflict had resolved itself within the first two years. Ideally, as the Piepers say, it would be better for parents and children 'not to act on the wish for more children until the parenting attention one child needs will not interfere with the parenting attention that is appropriate for the other'.[5]

Most children are pretty forgiving of their parents, provided they feel basically loved and loveable. It is almost inevitable that you will sometimes find yourself preferring one of your children to the other, and although this can be the source of great anxiety, shame and guilt, it is neither uncommon nor unreasonable: only the most saintly parent has no preference between a charming two-year-old and a bolshy four-year-old, between a bright-eyed chatty six-year-old and a tantruming three-year-old? Preferences tend to change with time, and different stages will be more or less testing. The main thing is not to display your feelings through favouritism. Love is not impervious to change, and it is natural to experience fluctuations in the intensity of your love for your children. Help yourself through the emotional demands of this period by being patient with yourself. If your children are very close in age, and if your first-born is not yet three, the emotional demands on you are bound to be high.

By no means all mothers will encounter problems in their feelings towards one or other of their children. But even when you have no difficulty feeling love for both your children, finding opportunities to express your love for your second child in the beady-eyed presence of your first is not always easy. In effect, the second-time mother must have her love affair with her new baby in public, a pretty unnerving experience at the best of times, not unlike being caught canoodling on the doorstep by your parents when you were a teenager. A friend of mine who has recently had her third child, confesses that she and her husband hold back during the day, 'but as soon as the boys are in bed we just fall on Isabelle, gazing and cooing at her to make up for lost time. It's really the only time we get to adore her unobserved.'

It's amazing how self-conscious a disapproving two-year-old can make you feel. Writer Helen Simpson describes this perfectly in a short story, 'Heavy Weather', in *Dear George,* in which a mother struggles to cope with her own feelings and the competing needs of her two small children.

> She was dismayed at how she had to treat him like some sort of fancy man to spare her daughter's feelings, affecting nonchalance when Lorna was around. She would fall on him for a quick mad embrace if the little girl left the room for a moment, only to spring apart guiltily at the sound of the returning Start-rites. The serrated teeth of remorse bit into her. In late pregnancy she had been so sandbaggd that she had had barely enough energy to crawl through the day, let alone reciprocate Lorna's incandescent two-year-old passion. 'She thought I'd come back to her as before once the baby arrived,' she said aloud. 'But I haven't.'

The emotions that children evoke are not constant and fixed, and perhaps one of the most invidious myths of mothering is that they should be. There are many ways of loving, and the best of them will still involve feelings that are, at times, a lot closer to hating than loving. The novelist Jennifer Uglow has described a fantasy of mothering 'an adoring tribe', at whose head she would sit, 'haloed in lamplight, dispensing *boeuf en daube*'. It's a fantasy that is, in some form or other, familiar to many of us. My own version, which accompanied me all though the years before I became a mother, had me smiling proudly at four adorable sons (four sons!) as they cavorted amicably on some windswept, but sunny beach. An intriguing aspect of these fantasies, it strikes me now, is how noiseless they were. Jennifer Uglow's adoring tribe don't utter a word; my cavorting boys are similarly minus their sound-track. Reality, of course, is seldom so serene and calm. 'Proximity to infants [draws] mothers into violent oscillations and extremes of feeling', writes Rozsika Parker in her book, *Torn in Two: The Experience of Maternal Ambivalence.*[6] 'The maternal ideal suggests that mother-love means *oneness*, while what mothers long for are loving moments of *at oneness*.'[7]

Loving children is not something that happens in a vacuum, and love is not something that flows smoothly and evenly as if from a well-plumbed tap. 'That one can feel so positive and so negative about the same experience is perhaps the most surprising contradiction of all,' writes Kate Figes in *Life After Birth*.

> As children grow and their demands mushroom, these feelings of hostility, ambiguity and being compromised grow too. They intensify and complicate and can swing from extreme hate to love in a matter of minutes. There are time when I don't want to hunt the house for a pencil sharpener, or draw Pingu for the hundredth time. There are times when I deeply resent scraping yet another plate of half-eaten tea into the dustbin, when I cannot summon up enthusiasm for yet another indifferent painting or laugh at yet another terrible joke. But that doesn't mean that I hate them, just because I hate 'it'.[8]

Actually, I think Figes is pulling the wool over her own eyes. I think at times we do indeed hate them. It is just too awful to admit this to ourselves. The biggest shock for many mothers is not only how much one loves one's own children, but also how intensely one can at times hate them. In *Of Woman Born*, the American poet, feminist and mother Adrienne Rich drew her classic portrait of how double-edged loving children can be:

> My children cause me the most exquisite suffering of which I have any experience. It is the suffering of ambivalence: the murderous alternation between bitter resentment and raw-edged nerves, and blissful gratification and tenderness. Sometimes I seem to myself, in my feelings toward these tiny guiltless beings, a monster of selfishness and intolerance. Their voices wear away at my nerves, their constant needs, above all their need for simplicity and patience, fill me with despair at my own failures, despair too at my fate, which is to serve a function for which I was not fitted… And yet at other times I am melted with the sense of their helpless, charming and quite irresistible beauty – their ability to go on loving and trusting – their staunchness and decency and unselfconsciousness. I love them. But it's in the enormity and inevitability of this love that the suffering lies.[9]

This is light years from the anodyne, sanitised vision of mother-love that so many of us still aspire to, and, more than twenty years after it was first written, it is still a far more accurate description of what many mothers-of-two go through – not all the time, of course, but more often than the uninitiated might think.

Love, love, love may be all you need, but not necessarily the exact same love at the exact same time. A woman's capacity for generosity, tolerance, patience and sensitivity towards her children will be affected by how other things are going in her life: how much sleep she's getting, how her marriage is going, whether she has any money to pay the bills, whether she has friends to talk to, or parents to help her. Her ability to love will be affected by her past experiences of being loved, as well as her present circumstances; it will be affected by the kind of woman she is, the values she holds, the expectations she has, the dreams she nurtures, both for herself and for her children.

We feel love differently at different times of our life and our children's lives; we also may, shock horror, discover that we love each of our children differently. It can be very hard to accept that your children are different, rouse different feelings in you and have different relationships with you. The traditional view of motherhood is that experience of one child carries over to the next, but as psychologist Penny Munn concludes from her own research, this is often not the case: 'A large part of mothering consists of discovering a unique individual and establishing a relationship with him or her. The individuality of the child plays a large part in the developing relationship between mother and infant, and this is a factor which is unaffected by parental learning. This is one aspect of childcare in which previous experience does not necessarily transfer from one child to the next, and may actually be unhelpful if expectations are inappropriate to the second child.'[10]

After their first child is born, many couples will have had to rethink their relationship with one another. The presence of that third person will have made a profound difference, on many levels, to the way you and your partner relate to each other. When you have your second child, your relationship will again need to adjust – and this time, so will the relationship between you and your first-born (and between your partner and his first-born). The arrival of the second child into a family means that now everyone will find themselves in a threesome at least some of the time – either as a parent and two children, or as a child and two parents. Many families go to great lengths to avoid the emotional complexities of these triangles by 'splitting' into pairs – 'he takes one child, I take the other', is a pattern described by many of the women I spoke to. In the short term this a sensible coping strategy, but in the long run that approach to life with two children, however initially attractive, is unsustainable.

One-to-one time – or 'man-to-man marking', as my partner calls it – should be seen as a temporary respite from, not an alternative to, the reality of multiple-parenting. Families who try and avoid the threesome by parenting in pairs are denying the reality of what they have created, its rewards as well as its challenges. Christopher Clulow, Director of the Tavistock Insitute for Marital Studies, takes a similar view: 'In psychoanalytic terms, the triangle is the fulcrum of personal development. When there is emphasis on exclusive twosomes, the triangle becomes problematic, and that usually happens when there are unresolved issues from the mother's or the father's past about the triangular relationship. They may be avoiding something that they haven't yet worked through from their own childhood.'

I am not saying that there is no place for one-to-one time. As Caroline and Mark found, one-to-one time is vitally important in the initial stages of adjusting to life with two children. And as children get older, it continues to be important, allowing you to give undivided attention to each child, without an audience looking on (and very often heckling). How to give each child the individual attention they need is is one of the particular difficulties facing single parents. You need time alone with your older child, especially during the first few years when your relationship has been hijacked – albeit unintentionally – by a second child. It allows you both to bank good experiences, which you can then set against the stress and strains of the adjustments you are both having to make. Equally, you need time alone with your new baby, time when you can coo and burble to your heart's content. If you're constantly scurrying to keep up with the needs and demands of two children, you'll only end up feeling you've given no real time or love to either. And after several days bouncing between two children, it's amazing how restful it can be to have just one to think about for an hour or so.

Loving children is always a two-way process: it consists not only of your feelings for them, but of their feelings for you, and most children, from a surprisingly early age, bring their own heady mix of emotions to the relationship. People say that it is the physical energy of small children that makes them so tiring, but it is much more to do with their emotional volatility – and the emotional agility their parents need to keep up. A day with an average two-year-old is like 24 hours of emotional circuit training, in which you lurch from delight to fear to annoyance to relief to exasperation to contentment, and back again. And then, of course, there are your children's feelings about each other to be hurled into the already fiercely simmering pot.

The ideal of steady, selfless maternal loving is still extraordinarily powerful in our culture, but it seldom exists in reality – just about manageable with one, perhaps, but impossible with two. We are happy to be flooded with the exquisite tenderness, or passion, or pride that our children can evoke, but far less comfortable with the frustration, the resentment, or with the 'unrecognisable, terrifying depths of anger', that Kate Figes describes, 'the fiery flash of murderous rage when a child's irrational recalcitrance drives me over the edge'.[11]

'The fit between our images of motherhood and the realities we confront is more uncomfortable than ever,' writes Susan Maushart. 'Today's media no longer glorify the housewife role. Instead, the spotlight has shifted to the celebrity Supermum, She-who-has-it-all. In the meantime, the "real mothering person" remains firmly in the closet.'[12] If some of us climb into that closet after our first child is born, many more of us clamber in after our second, as the impossibility of living up to those images becomes ever more apparent to us, if nobody else.

My tiny newborn is now a strapping three-year-old, whose favourite game is posting wetwipes down the loo (or maybe he just likes the man from Dyno-Rod), who can turn anything into a gun (and does), and who regards the word 'no' as a marvellous challenge. These days I cherish the moments of relative tranquillity with my daughter, whose movements seem so controlled and measured by comparison, who can read a book without destroying it, who stays still when I put her shoes on. After my son was born, it was a devastating blow to find my feelings for her so altered, a loss I was utterly unprepared for. It was the end of a magical love affair. For a long time I kept my feelings to myself, tried not to let them show, in particular tried not to let my daughter get a sense of anything being wrong. In the end, though, what helped us both was simply acknowledging what confusing times we were going through. One evening, about a year after having my second child, I was putting the children to bed and we were listening to a cassette of Woody Guthrie singing, 'Goodnight, Little Darling, Goodnight'. When the song finished, I leaned over and gave my daughter a kiss.

'And goodnight *my* little darling,' I said.

'Oh,' she said, most thoughtfully. 'Am I still your little darling? Even though I'm three and a half?'

'Yes,' I replied. 'You are still my little darling.'

It was a relief for us both to hear it, and to feel it was true.

'Sorry we're late, wardrobe crisis...'

Four

TEA FOR THREE

ving two children weren't enough to keep most of us fully occupied for the first year or so, there is also the not-so-small business of getting them both through the day. Having a second child is like trading the horse-and-cart you'd just mastered for an unruly coach-and-pair. In the headlong dash that passes for daily life, especially in the early years, two children means *at least* double the work. There are now two wriggly bodies to coax into clothes each morning; two breakfasts to be made, eaten and washed up; two sets of teeth to be brushed; two pairs of shoes to be tracked down – and four unwilling feet to be persuaded into those shoes once found; two (at least) favourite toys that must not be forgotten; two most precious beings to steer safely from front door to car or bus.

Children are dynamic, unpredictable, self-motivated individuals. From the moment our second child is born, we will be meeting two distinct, usually incompatible, often conflicting sets of needs, interests and demands, and having to do so simultaneously.

For the first few months after my second child was born, life seemed comprised of a bewildering switchback of highs and lows. I was enchanted by the new baby, full of tenderness for my disoriented two-year-old, and yet the combination of the two of them seemed overwhelming. Every day felt like an emotional assault course to be endured and survived. I had no history of post-natal depression, no ambivalent feelings about having a second child, no strong preferences for a girl or a boy. I had been eagerly anticipating the new baby's arrival, and yet within a few weeks home had turned into a kind of torture chamber in which I grew increasingly unhinged by the domestic equivalent of flashing lights, interrogating voices and dripping taps. Deep joy at the sight of the sleeping baby would be displaced a second later by a wave of ungovernable annoyance when my two-year-old refused to let me put her coat on. Mounting desperation on days when the baby wouldn't sleep or feed or be put down would abruptly dissolve to nothing at the sight of my daughter singing into the pram and the sound of the baby gurgling happily in response. I never knew what the next moment would bring. The bad moments were horrendous, although usually short-lived. The good moments were wonderful, but they were also fragile, precarious, easily shattered.

By the time the baby was six months old, I had recovered some semblance of equilibrium. It was six more months, though, before I felt able to go out of the house with both children without another adult to help. Even an outing to the post office was more than my stress levels could stand. The perils – real and imagined – of traffic, tantrums, rabid dogs and child abductors made facing our collective boredom threshold by staying at home a more attractive option.

I was exhausted by broken nights and constant demands, and since my daughter had long ago dropped a daytime nap there was no chance of catching up when the baby dozed off. Roads, shops, parks, in fact any open space, presented a challenge to my temper and my pelvic floor that neither could yet rise to. I simply didn't have the emotional or physical resilience to cope with her and him and the great outdoors. So we stayed at home instead. The baby was coming up for his first birthday before I stopped feeling quite so frazzled, regained some of my old energy, recovered a modicum of resourcefulness in my dealings with my first-born. Taking them both swimming for the first time when the younger one was 14 months was a personal triumph equivalent to winning an Olympic Gold.

Even after *two* years of intensive training, there were still days when I would find the most basic aspects of life with two small children entirely beyond me. The morning 'routine' frequently bordered on the farcical. Things might get off to a deceptively good start if my daughter decided to get dressed by herself, but then I'd discover that she'd forgotten to put on any knickers. By the time I'd persuaded her to take her tights off again in order to put some pants on, she'd have decided that she wanted a different pair of tights and a different pair of shoes, and maybe a hair band, and could I put her hair in a plait? I'd give way on the tights, insist on the shoes, take five minutes to find the hairbrush, and fail entirely to locate the right hairband. ('NO, mummy! It's GOT to be the blue one! The red one doesn't GO!') I'd then try to get myself dressed, which could easily take a whole half hour (in contrast to the scheduled 30 seconds) on account of both children making constant, conflicting demands, so that I'd get distracted, put on a white top over a black bra, then a blue sock with a black one, then forget where I'd put my shoes, then lose the second black sock I'd just found. I'd try going to a different room to dress but the children would follow, taking it in turns to need me urgently in order to stop a fight, save their lives, prevent a tantrum. Most mornings it was like a Benny Hill sketch with people in various states of undress chasing each other along hallways and up and down stairs. Finally I'd get myself and my daughter dressed and turn to the toddler. Having watched our shenanigans cheerfully enough up until this point, he'd now throw a major fit and utterly refuse to co-operate with the task of taking off his pyjamas, changing his nappy, putting on a new nappy/socks/T-shirt/trousers/jumper and shoes. By the time I'd wrestled a screaming, writhing, furious boy into his clothes, my once white shirt would be smeared in snot, marmite and banana. So it was back to my bedroom to change. Some days we'd start getting dressed at eight o'clock and not finish until nearly ten, with the prospect of teeth-brushing and coats still ahead, and nursery having opened at nine.

With two children, I discovered, things had to go only slightly wrong to get completely out of hand. Had I planned better – set out all our clothes the night before, got up half an hour earlier, wiped the toddler's face before trying to dress him – maybe things would have gone more smoothly, but maybe they wouldn't, and maybe I'd have been born with a halo instead of a guilt complex.

It is the feeling of being pulled in two opposing directions that can make looking after two young children so stressful, and so normal, particularly at the beginning. It's not just a case of now having two children who need daytime naps, but having two children who may need daytime naps at very different times of the day. It's not just a case of now having two children to take to the swings, but having two children who want to go there at different speeds, do different things when they get there (both requiring your supervision) and have different views from each other, and you, about when is the right time to go home again. Even finding a baby-and-toddler group that fits in with the hours your older child is at nursery can be a challenge, particularly when those hours are the only time you have in the whole day for all the errands that just can't be done with two children in reluctant, rebellious tow. 'The tasks of mothering are not increased additively with each birth,' according to Penny Munn, 'but rather multiply in complexity.'[1]

The tasks of mothering do indeed 'multiply in complexity', and furthermore the nature of those tasks keeps changing as the children themselves change. The placid baby becomes a determined toddler; the accepting two-year-old becomes a bolshy three-year-old. No sooner have we adjusted ourselves to one stage than our children leap on to the next. An experienced health visitor told me she had lost count of the number of times she has heard mothers exclaiming enthusiastically, a week after having their second child, that their first child was thrilled with the baby and that everything was going fine. 'They think they've cracked it and there is nothing more to worry about! It's amazing how few parents are able to see that the newborn baby won't stay newborn forever, and that the older child may be a lot less thrilled once the baby is crawling around and grabbing his toys.'

Every mother-of-two will agree that one can't hope to please all of the people all of the time. With more than one child to care for, child-centred approaches to bringing up children come under serious strain: you can fit in with one child easily enough, but how do you accommodate two, when so often their needs are different? I wholeheartedly agree with Deborah Jackson when she argues in her book *Do Not Disturb* that we often hurry children unnecessarily, but with two children, you simply cannot keep everyone happy. How do you feed wholesome gloop to the baby in a serene and loving fashion when your three-year-old is so determined to wind you up that she is scaling the kitchen cupboards to get at the butter dish you moved out of her reach five minutes earlier? How do you go at the snail's pace of a toddler and the lightning speed of a four-year-old? How do you chill out while one finishes building his version of the Eiffel Tower, when the other is frantic to go out on her new bike? How do you do jigsaw puzzles with one, when the other keeps walking off with half the pieces?

The First Four Months

Immediately after our second child is born, our concerns are usually focused on how our first-born is reacting to the new arrival, rather than on how we ourselves are getting on. Most mothers watch their first-born anxiously during these early days for signs of disturbance, and usually make every effort to soften the blow of having just produced a lifelong rival and competitor. They are usually pleasantly surprised by how well their first child takes to his or her sibling. In fact, early reactions to a new baby are much more likely to be targeted at you and your partner than at the baby. 'The funny thing was that Zoe was absolutely sweet with the baby,' recalls Deborah. 'She brought toys for Caitlin to look at, sang songs to her, and wanted to hold her. It was very touching. But at the same time she was a real handful. We had lots of tantrums in the first few weeks, and even though she'd been potty-trained since she was two, there were suddenly lots of "accidents", usually when I was feeding Caitlin.'

Setbacks with toilet training are very common. One study found that nearly 50 per cent of first-born children who'd previously been toilet-trained started wetting themselves again after the arrival of a new baby.[2] First-borns are also likely to be more demanding and clingy than usual. (Well, wouldn't you be?) However easy your second baby, it will still be taking up a lot of your time and attention, and even when the baby's sleeping, you may be too zonked to feel like playing hide-and-seek, or making fairy cakes, or even reading Peter Rabbit for what seems like the 500th time.

Sheer fatigue is often what prevents mothers from doing the things they know would make a difference, and unfortunately the more tired you are, the more your first-born is likely to play up. This can rapidly set up a vicious cycle, as Judy Dunn found. 'Mothers who reported the greatest feelings of tiredness and depression had first-born children who showed the greatest levels of distress and disturbance after the birth.'[3] This was certainly part of the problem for Deborah. 'After Caitlin was born, Zoe started waking at night again, and by the time she was three weeks old both children were waking several times every night. It was absolutely exhausting – and it went on like that for months and months and months. I could see very well that Zoe was feeling insecure and needed me to be extra loving and reassuring, but a lot of the time I was too tired to do anything about it. Whenever I got the baby off to sleep I just needed to crash out myself. I knew what she needed from me, but I didn't have the energy to provide it.'

In the first weeks after the arrival of a sibling, many first-borns resort to a level of quite deliberate naughtiness that their mothers have never seen before. I remember going to visit a friend when her second child was five days old. We were in the living-room looking at the baby and chatting, when we realised her two-year-old had disappeared. We found her a few moments later in the hallway, where she was quietly and efficiently smearing zinc and caster oil cream all over the walls. It was a rented house and my friend had always been very firm about not drawing on the walls. Her daughter knew it was one of the very naughtiest things she could do. Her silent protest left us in no doubt at all about her views on the new baby.

Judy Dunn observed a marked increase in exactly this kind of deliberate naughtiness in the first few weeks after the birth of a second child. 'In these early weeks, very many children will repeatedly do exactly what they have been told not to do… Wallpaper was systematically ripped from the wall, baby's bath was deliberately tipped over on the floor, the television the mother was watching was repeatedly switched off, a whole line of clean laundry was let down into the mud – the ingenuity of the actions was remarkable.'[4] Dunn and her colleagues watched toddlers and pre-schoolers expertly pick out the one thing that was guaranteed to wind up their parent. The mothers were asked what behaviour they had found most annoying in their first-born before the new baby was born: 'What we found was that after the new baby arrived, there was a sudden escalation of precisely those actions that the mothers had particularly minded.'[5] In other words, children draw on their intimate knowledge of their parents' likes and dislikes – and hone in on the latter with unerring accuracy. 'In response, the first-born always got attention, but most often it was irritation rather than reassurance.' Children very quickly get caught in a negative spiral of naughtiness, and overstretched parents can unwittingly exacerbate the problem by getting angry.

Affection and attention are closely linked in the minds of young children, and throughout childhood children will need our attention most when our supply of the stuff is at its lowest. Now is one of those times. Consider the way that all too many grown men and women behave when there's a temporary shortage of petrol, and you can see that many of us don't grow out of this response. Spasms of naughtiness from children who have just become siblings are the equivalent of 'panic buying'. Look at it from their point of view: a most vital commodity is suddenly in short supply; can you blame them for trying to stock up? Their actions may seem like gross provocation to you, but to children, they are 'affection raids'.

It is a rare and fortunate first-born who does not experience some degree of attention-deficit after the birth of a second child. For most children, the decline in attention is swift and steep and irreversible. Your bemused first-born has never had to work so hard for your attention in his or her life. No wonder he or she doesn't always choose the best way of getting it, as Deborah recalls: 'Caitlin was a month old, and I'd had one of those awful mornings when she wouldn't settle and I couldn't get on with anything. Zoe was getting more and more frantic, waiting for me to get round to her. Every time I was about to, Caitlin would start crying again and I'd have to attend to her instead. Finally, at about 3.00 in the afternoon, she went off to sleep, and I was able to sit down with Zoe to read her a story. We'd only been sitting there a few moments and I felt this warm wet patch spreading across my lap and I realised she'd wet herself, and me, and the sofa. I lost my temper completely and shouted at her for being so stupid. All I could think of was how much extra work she'd just caused me – washing her, washing the sofa covers, washing the floor, washing myself. It was the last straw. But afterwards I was thinking about it again and realised that probably the reason she'd sat there and wet herself was because she hadn't wanted to interrupt the story – and the cuddle – when she'd had to wait so long for it. I felt really ashamed of myself for getting so cross. At the time, though, all I could see was how we'd just lost another chance to sit down and do something enjoyable together.'

The kind of 'naughtiness' directly brought on by the birth of a younger sibling is extremely taxing to parents, but needs to be understood for what it really is: both an expression of confusion and a plea for more of your attention. The only effective response, as well as the only compassionate one, is to try and give them what they're searching for. Hard as it may be, setting aside at least 15 minutes of focused time each day for your older child will be of more benefit to you both than taking a 'firm line', which is akin to punishing them for needing you, or displaying a superhuman degree of tolerance, which your child may interpret as you not caring that they need you.

Alongside deliberate naughtiness, but requiring a slightly different response, is another common form of misbehaviour: systematic trickiness. This tends to occur around routine but essential daily activities, such as dressing, eating, getting into car seats and pushchairs, and going to bed. Ruth, mother of four-year-old Hannah and two-year-old Rachel, found that immediately after her second child was born, this was one of the most trying things she had to deal with: 'Hannah almost drove me mad after Rachel was born with her fussing about clothes. She would insist on dressing herself in bizarre and impractical things, like a thin cotton dress and short socks on a freezing cold winter's day. The baby was usually screaming miserably by the time we'd agreed what Hannah was going to wear, and then at the last moment she'd decide to change into something completely different and we'd have to start all over again. It took every shred of my patience not to strangle her at times!'

Trickiness may also take the form of veering from one parent to another, insisting that mummy picks her up, then screaming that no, it must be daddy who carries her. Similarly, you may find your older child suddenly refusing to go to a person they usually like. It is also very common for first-born children to want to be babied themselves. Persuading your older child to get out of the pram/cot/Moses basket so you can put the baby in it is an experience with which most new mothers-of-two will be familiar. Your first-born, similarly, may decide he wants to breast-feed/drink out of a bottle/have a pacifier/wear nappies/eat baby food. I remember my two-and-a-half-year-old squeezing herself into her baby brother's snow suit, and exclaiming with delight, 'Look, it fits me!', and insisting on wearing it for the rest of the day, regardless of the fact that the sleeves only reached to her elbows and the legs only reached to her knees.

Fussing, whinging, and generally being as awkward as it is possible to be, are all normal and usually short-lived reactions. Something like 15 per cent of first-borns will react the other way and become withdrawn after the birth of second child. It is also very common for first-born children to develop irrational fears, one or two months after their sibling is born. None of these behaviours are in themselves indications of future problems, and they will not usually last longer than about six months.

Maddening as they are, try to remind yourself that this kind of behaviour is invariably a symptom of insecurity, a way of expressing just how 'out of joint' their world has suddenly become since the birth of their younger sibling. Making a fuss about clothes or food or bedtime is a way of saying: 'Things feel different and I'm not sure I like it.' Asserting his or her own ideas about how the world should be run is a form of protest about the changes that have taken place that he or she can't quite understand and can't do anything about. Where possible, take pre-emptive action: put a potty/book/drink by the sofa when you're breast-feeding; take your older child to use the loo before you sit down to feed the baby. Try not to reward irritating behaviour with irritated attention – it's better to ignore misbehaviour in the first few weeks. Instead, try very hard to identify good behaviour in your first-born, focus on the things you're pleased with, for example, the way your older child made the baby smile, or the lovely game he or she played with her teddies, or the way he or she helped you set the table for lunch. Try to make as much time as possible for your first-born, preferably time alone. Even taking the older one with you to the supermarket will be appreciated.

Making time to go on real treats and outings alone with your older child will not only make up to them for the genuine attention-deficit they are suffering, but will also help you to see them as a person in their own right, who is not just there to make looking after the baby as difficult as possible. Go out to a café together, go to the library, go to the museum and look at the dinosaur skeletons, go to an art gallery and look at the paintings, go the station and look at the trains.

The only kind of treat that won't work is the present that is actually a poorly disguised fob-off. In other words, the present that makes you feel better about how little time you're spending with your first-born, the present that is also intended to keep your older child occupied without any extra involvement from you. This is not a treat, it is gift-wrapped guilt. You know it (or you should do) and so at one level or another does your child.

Helping Your First-born To Adjust

- Lavish attention and affection on your older child. The baby won't mind who is providing the kisses and cuddles, but your first-born wants *you*.
- Encourage visitors to pay attention to your first-born as well as the new baby. Suggest visitors bring something for both children, not just the newborn.
- Let your older child 'help' with the baby, by fetching nappies or clothing. Don't be too exacting.
- Expect a 'reaction' from your first-born. Acting out and acting up are normal and common.
- Ignore deliberate naughtiness in the first few weeks.
- Be extra tolerant about whining, fussing and other annoying behaviour.
- Avoid imposing your views and feelings about the new baby on to its older sibling. Your older child may really have wanted a little brother and be bitterly disappointed by the arrival of a sister; maybe your older child is upset that the baby doesn't look like her dolls.
- Never dismiss or laugh at your child's viewpoint.
- Acknowledge your first-born's feelings. When she says she hates the baby, that is how she is feeling. Without criticising or judging, translate back to your child what she is trying to express. 'It sounds as if you're upset that the baby is taking up so much of my attention.' 'You sound as if you're angry that I can't play with you as much as before.' Articulating your child's feelings in this way will help him to understand and feel less overwhelmed by them.
- Make time to do things alone with your older child; they need and will relish the undivided attention.
- Check that your expectations of your older child are appropriate. Don't expect your first-born to 'grow up overnight'.
- Allow at least a year for your older child to adjust fully to the arrival of a sibling.

With so much concern focused on how your older child may react immediately before and after the birth, we often forget to factor the new baby into our equations. A difficult baby, whether it's your first or your second, is always intensely demoralising for its parents, especially if it comes after an easier one. Almost nothing compares with the emotional and mental torment of a baby that won't settle, won't feed, won't sleep. The combination of a difficult baby and a displaced first-born can be a real killer, even when both children are behaving in a perfectly normal way for their age. Difficult babies create enormous stress for everyone in the family – and then, of course, respond to the stress by being even more difficult.

If your second child is particularly demanding, it is vitally important that you get time alone with your older child and time off from both children. Don't suffer in silence. Ask your GP or health visitor for help, or, if you don't want to talk to them, organisations like Cry-sis and Parentline Plus run free, confidential telephone helplines, and can provide much needed moral and practical support. (*See* Help & Advice, p.214.) Parentline Plus takes calls from thousands of parents each year, runs parenting courses round the country, and can refer you to other relevant organisations in your area. Another option is Home Start, a nationwide organisation that runs a free service of trained volunteers who will visit you at home on a regular basis and provide friendship, practical help and emotional support. If broken nights are a particular problem, you might want to consider hiring in help at night. Most good nanny agencies can supply maternity nurses to help with newborns. Night Nannies is a London-based company specialising in this area. It provides qualified nannies from 9.00pm to 7.00am who are specially trained to help settle young children into good sleeping habits.

If there's one thing motherhood teaches us, it's that time usually brings the changes we long for. If there's one thing motherhood seems not to teach us, however, it's that sitting it out in stoical silence is both unhelpful and unnecessary. Health visitors report that second-time mothers are even more reluctant to admit problems than first-time mothers, and take far longer to seek help they may badly need. This is partly due to the power of what Jayne Buxton calls 'the myth of the earth mother', which says we should be blissfully contented with our small brood about our knees, and feel ashamed if we're not.[6] Unreasonable expectations of ourselves may be one reason we hold off getting help when we need it, but another reason why we wait until we're desperate to admit anything is wrong, is that the worse things get, the harder it is to sound the alarm. Most people without children simply have no idea what an impressive degree of will-power, stamina and ingenuity are demonstrated day after day after day by millions of women around the world as they manoeuvre two small children and themselves out of a house and into the great wide world. When things aren't going smoothly, the combination of waning self-confidence and mounting desperation can make 'help', not to mention the front door, seem impossibly far off. Getting out of the house or even getting to the phone can seem beyond one's capabilities.

Second time round, women are inclined to look at other women and think to themselves, 'Well, she's coping. What's the matter with me?', and then retreat behind their front doors, so that at least no one else will see them not coping. In fact, physical and psychological problems can just as easily occur after your second child comes along, and certain problems will occur only for the first time this time, since they may be specifically connected to the task of looking after two children as opposed to one. With studies suggesting that nearly half of all mothers with children under five experience emotional distress, either regularly or continually, and that 30 to 80 per cent of mothers of under-fives suffer from mild depression, we should at least feel confident that we are not alone, however much it may feel like it at times.

A number of organisations exist to support parents with young children, such as Newpin, Home Start, Meet-a-Mum Association and Pippin. All provide free help in various forms. Home Start sees itself as providing the sort of informal support that many people would once have got from their extended family. 'We are definitely not here to tell people how they should be parents,' insists Brian Waller, director of Home Start. 'We're at the friendship end of the spectrum. We're fulfilling the kinds of roles that grandparents and other relations used to provide.'

Home Start runs local schemes all over the country, and is growing fast: it currently has around 7,000 volunteers working in nearly 300 community-based programmes. Volunteers are all parents themselves and will visit a family on a regular basis, usually once a week for a few hours for as long as the family wants. The service is confidential and, as Waller emphasises, not driven by any particular ideology of parenting, but rather a belief in the value of friendship and company. 'We're not social workers and we're not trained counsellors. We just try to offer the kind of help and care that a friend or relative would offer. A great many of the families who come to us are having problems with isolation and basic lack of support. It's a major problem for many people today. Isolation and depression aren't just found on council estates, they're just as common in leafy suburbs.'

Demand for Home Start's service is growing all the time: the organisation is currently opening a new local scheme every ten days in response to demand. When you haven't talked to another adult all week, as Home Start has shown, having a volunteer coming round is a lifeline. An evaluation of Home Start schemes in Scotland showed that the service is helping people in very tangible ways. Families reported feeling more confident, handling problems with their children better, feeling physically better, coming off medication and enjoying improved self-esteem. It had a positive impact on parental health and self-esteem and on behavioural problems in children. Objective assessments of these families supported their view.

The success of Home Start lies in its simplicity. Sometimes all volunteers will do is go round and have a chat, or they may help in more practical ways, by taking children to the park, helping with the shopping, or letting a sleep-deprived mother take a nap. A woman of triplets contacted Home Start for support when her children were six months old. She used the time to have a bath in peace once a week. It may seem a small thing, but for her it made a big impact.'

I didn't know about Home Start when I was slowly going stir-crazy at home with my children when they were very young. Or rather I had seen a leaflet, but thought it was publicising some kind of coffee morning circuit. Had I realised that here was an organisation that might have helped me to catch up on some desperately needed sleep once a week, I'd have rung them like a shot. Instead, I kept up the appearance of coping for as long as possible (about six months), then took the time-honoured route of bursting into tears all over my GP, who seemed somewhat embarrassed by my incoherent blubbering, but alerted the health visitor. She came to see me once a week for the next six weeks at home, ostensibly to talk about my second child's night-time antics. The extent to which I depended on these low-key weekly visits was not apparent to me at the time, but looking back I can see how significant they were. One week the health visitor got caught in traffic and was late. My stress levels escalated with each minute. When she finally turned up, all of ten minutes behind time, I fell upon her with a ferocity born of desperation. The dividing line between 'just about OK' and 'totally panic-stricken' at that stage in my life was very thin indeed. Regular support helped me turn the corner.

If you are finding your second child or the combination of two children hard going, it is crucial to carve out some time for yourself, away from children (whether you spend it alone, with your partner or with friends). Don't wait for things to get better or settle down; don't tell yourself that you must be doing something wrong or that it's all your fault – just drag yourself to the phone, ring your health visitor or GP and tell them what's going on. They will be able to arrange a referral or some kind of treatment.

Four Months to a Year

After three or four months, the baby will usually be getting easier, more into a routine of feeding and sleeping, less prone to colic and generally more predictable. Developmental changes in the baby at around four to six months also begin to make it easier to establish some routines and strategies for meeting both children's needs.

Fiona, mother of Phoebe and Luke, found that life with two children became much more manageable once her youngest reached six months. 'Luke was a very restless small baby who never slept in the day for more than 20 minutes or so. The first couple of months were extremely difficult for me and for Phoebe, who never seemed to get any proper time with me. The only time Phoebe got real attention was when Peter got home from work. They became very close during those weeks, and I sometimes found that difficult to handle too! I hated the feeling that Phoebe was slipping away from me. When Luke was six months old, he at last got into a routine of having an hour's nap every afternoon, which continued until he was two and a half. It was my complete saving. I had to be very strict with myself not to fritter away the time washing up and tidying, and it was a great temptation just to put Phoebe in front of a video and enjoy the peace and quiet. Having that little bit of time to do things together in a quiet, concentrated way was so important.'

Even if your baby does not develop a regular daytime sleep, it should still become easier as the months pass to get some time away, either on your own, or with your older child, by leaving the baby for an hour with a friend or relative, or paying someone to come in. One woman – a full-time, at-home mother-of-three – arranged for a babysitter to come in three afternoons a week from 5.00pm until 7.00pm, letting her off what every parent knows are the worst two hours of the day. Caroline, mother of Tom and Bridget, employed a nanny when Bridget was four months old, and found this made a significant difference to the tenor of her day: 'Tom always had a daytime sleep right up until he was two and a half, and I just expected that my second would too, but Bridget was a little live-wire from the word go, and never slept regularly during the day. It was almost impossible to find time to concentrate on Tom. When Bridget was four months old, Lynne started working for us, three days a week. I could leave Bridget at home with Lynne while I took Tom to nursery school on my way to work. It wasn't much, but it was a huge relief. Even that little bit of time alone together made a big difference. He really loved it, and so did I.'

The great see-saw of family life does not stay still for long, however, and just as your baby begins to settle down into more of a routine, your older child often seizes the chance to find new ways of testing your devotion. It is very common for parents to find their first-born more stressful four months after the birth of a second child than they were after one.[7] Many parents actually find their first-born remains the major source of stress for up to a year. Contrariness, whinging and fussing, for example, which can all start soon after the birth, may not let up until the baby is nine months old. Night-time waking and setbacks with toilet training may take up to six months to resolve themselves, although the encouraging evidence is that these kinds of problems usually do sort themselves out, providing you can stay calm and patient in the meantime.

After about four months, you may also be witnessing some signs of jealousy and aggression directed at the baby for the first time, such as prodding, pinching, snatching and even outright hitting. One in three first-born children is likely to develop these kinds of worries and phobias at some time in the first year. As Deborah discovered, the intensity of these anxieties can be pretty shocking for parents: 'Zoe had been riding on the back of our bikes since she was a baby, but about two months after Caitlin was born, she suddenly started refusing to get into her bike seat. She would scream and scream, and was obviously really frightened. Nothing we could say or do made any difference. That went on for about a month, and then it stopped as suddenly as it had started.' Other children may develop a fear of water, and not want to be bathed, or they may become frightened of the dark, or become very anxious about losing things, or getting hurt. One little boy of two developed a powerful fear of an invisible tiger that lived in his bedroom. At bedtime he would cling and cling to his mother or father, genuinely terrified. His parents finally solved the problem when they removed the boy's cot quilt, which was decorated with pictures of animals, including a tiger.

However testing and aggravating your older child's behaviour is, try to remember, as before, that he or she is still in the process of adjusting to the momentous change of becoming and having a sibling. Irrational fears and obsessions reflect insecurity rather than a desire to make your life difficult. Try to respond with affection and tolerance, rather than anger or anxiety. As far as possible, respect your child's fear, avoid situations that cause him or her anxiety, and try to remember that the problem is in all likelihood temporary. Similarly, aggressive or provocative behaviour should be treated firmly, but calmly, and the underlying expression of anxiety that it conveys should be responded to with warmth and reassurance, rather than punishment.

Children – like all of us – need to be encouraged and praised for doing things well and getting things right. It is very easy to focus on bad behaviour and let the good behaviour go unmentioned. Instead, reverse the pattern by identifying and personalising good behaviour – 'you did that really well', 'that's a lovely picture you've drawn', 'thank you for putting your clothes away', 'your help really made a difference', 'I was very proud of you when…' Being firm about behaviour you dislike is important, but make it clear that it is the behaviour that you dislike, not the child. Labelling children as bad/naughty/lazy/clumsy/selfish is unhelpful – they will simply do their best to live down to your expectations.

Sadly, we praise children less and less as they get older, filling their heads instead with negative messages. 'Why do you have to be so messy?' 'Don't be so selfish.' 'You're the laziest child I've ever known.' Studies have shown that the arrival of a second child tends to coincide with a rise in the number of times a day a first child is criticised and a drop in the number of times a day a first child is praised, kissed and cuddled. Talk about bad timing. But praising children is not just a matter of a distracted 'well done', or 'that's great'. To be effective, praise has to be a bit more thoughtful and sincere than that. There are two types of praise: praise for being and praise for doing. The first tells your child that you value them for who they are, that you're glad to have them in your life. The second tells your child that you appreciate their behaviour or achievements or efforts. Children need praise on a regular (daily) basis both for being and for doing.

Children who are praised frequently and effectively do not become spoiled or conceited; instead, they internalise these positive messages and feel confident, loved and appreciated. Plenty of praise now leads to good self-esteem later.

Effective Praise and Encouraging Encouragement

- Give undivided attention. You can't praise effectively while also watching TV, reading the paper or surfing the Internet.
- Move closer to the child. Squat, bend or kneel so you're at the child's level.
- Make eye contact and look pleased and interested.
- Make physical contact to convey to your child that you are really engaged.
- Be specific about what it is you are praising. For example, if your child has put away her toys, instead of a vague 'That's good', spell it out by saying, 'You've done a really good job of tidying up your toys.'
- Avoid mixing praise with criticism, advice or comparisons. 'You've tidied your toys up much better tonight'; 'You've tidied up very well, but it's better not to mix the lego and the train track.' 'Well done! You've tidied your toys much better than your brother.' These are all back-handers and don't count.

(Adapted from the Family Links Nurturing Programme.)

Most of the difficulties that parents experience with their first-born in the year after the arrival of a second child are normal and temporary: not signs of poor adjustment, but symptoms of normal adjustment. The real problem is that our expectations of how long these normal reactions should go on for are often wildly unrealistic. Most parents are patient and understanding with their first child for the first couple of months after their second child is born. This is not usually nearly long enough. 'As the months go by,' writes Judy Dunn, 'your first-born's need for attention and reassurance of your continued love can show up in ways that may strike you as odd and even rather perverse. Since things seem to have settled down somewhat, you may not initially connect these behaviours with the baby's presence, but that is often what underlies them.'[8]

Robert Stewart's study of 40 couples who'd just had their second child amply supports Dunn's view. Stewart and his colleagues found the mothers in their study were very satisfied with their first-born child immediately after their second child's birth, but became increasingly dissatisfied with their first-born child as the year went on. When the researchers looked at what these children were actually doing, it seemed to them that the mothers' annoyance was out of all proportion to the children's behaviour. The researchers concluded that mothers were simply not allowing enough time for the older child to adjust to having a younger sibling. Or, rather, they expected the adjustment to happen once, at the very beginning, whereas in fact the older child needed to keep on adjusting as the baby itself changed and was able to make more and more impact on the older child's world, and to claim more and more attention from parents. Throughout the first year, older children have to keep 'altering their strategies to regain or maintain parental involvement'.[9] As the baby becomes more active, and more of a threat, the older child's need for support and understanding increases, but parents, and particularly mothers, are often unaware of this. Instead, mothers tend to become much less patient with their first-born as time goes on. Many simply assume that their older child should have finished adjusting by now, and no longer deserve the tolerance they readily gave in the early weeks. This mismatch between older children's needs and mothers' assumptions is very common and greatly adds to the strain on both.

The only safe ruling is this: don't expect to have seen it all in the first month or two. Some reactions to becoming and getting a sibling are slower to emerge than others, and some children will take longer to work through their feelings than others. Furthermore, different types of children will combine in different ways, and some combinations will make life easier for parents than others. One woman I spoke to had a strong-willed daughter followed by an easy-going son. Another had two boys who had both slept for two hours morning and afternoon throughout their first year of life. A third had an amenable boy followed by an energetic headstrong girl. A fourth had two bright, but physically docile girls. Jane, a musician in her late thirties, married to an historian, had a very easy girl, followed by a very difficult one. 'Helena was the most tranquil baby imaginable, but Jessica was quite the opposite. She cried a lot and was difficult to settle. We moved house a month after she was born and so everything was in turmoil at home, and I found it completely impossible to keep both girls happy at once. There was nothing they both wanted to do at once. It was just awful, for months and months. Now of course it's completely different. Helena is seven and Jessica is nearly six and they play together all the time.'

As the weeks turn into months, mothering two children is increasingly about managing the relationship between them. By the time your younger child is eight months old, you will be managing not only two very different children, each with their own physical, emotional and psychological needs, but also an increasingly fiery relationship between them. By eight months, the baby is starting to understand how to get attention, and is also likely to be moving around and able to trespass on the older child's territory: it is fast becoming a physical and emotional competitor. By eight months, the baby is no longer a passive recipient of your attention, but an active and skilful manipulator of your attention. Another year and that baby will be fast turning into a determined toddler, 'likely to offer both deliberate interference with an older child's play and deliberate naughtiness to a mother'. As this transformation occurs, starting at around eight months, conflict between siblings begins to escalate, and demands on the mother soar. According to Penny Munn, 'It is at this point – when the second child can no longer be accommodated as an infant – that the discrepancy between the reality of mothering two children and the model based on mothering one child is at its height.'[10]

Between eight months and a year, demands on the mother, in the words of one health visitor, 'escalate monumentally'. Robert Stewart found that satisfaction in second-time mothers nose-dived at around eight months, and that, 'By 12 months postpartum, the demandingness of the first-born… was perceived as a major source of stress by many of the parents.'[11] It may be that this is when the physical demands are at a maximum and help from others is at a minimum. You may still feel very restricted in what you can do and where you can go at this stage. You may also recently have gone back to work.

Physically, your children will slowly become less dependent on you, especially once your younger child gets into his second year, but individually and collectively children will become more intense and demanding before they become less so. As Kate Figes explains very well in *Life After Birth*: 'It is the constant cycle of persuasion, psychological bolstering and lion-taming that makes motherhood so tiring that it can be hard at times to find the joy. When both children were small there were days when I felt as if I was sinking into the role of the nagging grumpy mother that I swore to myself I would never ever be, because the only words I ever seemed to utter were orders – pick that up, please, don't kick that chair, leave her alone… It is the very repetitive constancy of motherhood that women find so draining and which often makes them feel depressed or angry, for exhaustion distorts reality.'[12]

As time goes on, the problems that many mothers encounter with their children will gradually change, but the overall impact of having two children may not yet feel appreciably easier. Penny Munn concludes from her observations of 50 second-time mothers that the experience of mothering two children was influenced by 'a series of developmental events occurring in the younger child, rather than a discrete event such as the arrival of a new baby, or the start of full-time schooling'.[13] It is not until your younger child is two and a half or three that their increasing autonomy and competence will begin to make life significantly easier for you. This is when many mothers begin to feel that they are 'emerging', 'coming out the other side'.

It's easy with two children to lose sight of their individuality and just see them as items to be got through the day. It's easy to lose sight of the very different stages two children can be at, and the very different needs and interests they may have. It's also hard to keep track of the way in which those needs and interests keep changing. With my daughter, when it was just my daughter, I was finely tuned to every new verbal, mental or physical skill she acquired. My son, by contrast, was approaching his second birthday before he even saw a jigsaw, because I'd not really noticed that he was old enough for such things.

Keeping pace with the different and changing needs of two children requires a cool head and an even temper – attributes not always in generous supply among parents of under-fives. It is all too easy to expect your first-born to be more grown up than he or she really is, and to expect your second-born to be less able. Jane, mother of Helena and Jessica, thinks this was the cause of much unnecessary tension when her children were younger: 'Looking back I can see that so many of the flare-ups that we had in the first couple of years were because I couldn't see how young Helena still was. I saw Jessie as the little one and just didn't make enough allowances for Helena. I expected her to grow up very fast, and tended to see her as older than her age. I'd get furious when she dawdled over putting her shoes on in the morning, and I remember being really taken aback one day when I heard another mother saying she didn't expect her child to be able to put his own shoes on until he started school.'

Your expectations of your younger child may also be unrealistic. Newborn babies do cry a lot; one-year-olds do cling and scream when you leave the room without them (psychologists call this 'separation anxiety', mothers simply call it 'hell'); toddlers do throw tantrums several times a day; two-and-a-half-year-olds do hold very strong opinions about important matters, such as which pyjama top they're going to wear tonight, and they tend to have more stamina for getting their way than you do for getting yours. It helps to be aware of behaviour that is developmentally appropriate at different stages: it won't change the behaviour itself, but it may make it easier for you to understand why your child is behaving in a certain way, and to remember that it is temporary. When my husband one morning snapped with exasperation at our daughter, 'Come on! For heaven's sake, put your coat on! You're four now!', she protested indignantly, 'But, Daddy, I've never been four before.'

Inevitably, there will be days when keeping both children even reasonably happy just seems impossible. In the first few years, even a two-year age gap can set your children light years apart developmentally speaking. A four-year-old is at the stage when she can lose herself for hours in an imaginative game, while her two-year-old brother may still find throwing Lego more interesting than building with it. She will be understandably annoyed when he 'helps' her make a castle by removing half the pieces she's just put in place, irritated when the fat little fist that you find so adorable accidentally knocks over the castle keep, and infuriated when that same fist hijacks a handful of the 'little people' that she's just carefully arranged. He, on the other hand, is understandably frustrated by only being allowed to spectate. Sooner or later he will try to liven things up by clonking her with the toy kettle – that always gets an interesting reaction, he finds.

To the uninitiated the solution may appear obvious: separate activities. But they don't work for long either. The unspoken rule upheld by children under five seems to be congregate and conflagrate. Maddeningly, they always want to be doing what the other one is doing (usually for no other reason than that you are doing it with them). How many mothers have found themselves playing ball with the baby to stop him crawling over to the older child's dolls' party, only to watch the older child decide she wants to play ball too, but without letting the baby have a turn? It is amazing how hard it can be to attract a child's attention when you want to, but how easy when you don't. Amazing too how a child of any age can sense you so much as thinking about giving attention to someone else, especially if they're a sibling. I do have friends who can make complicated cardboard spaceships with their pre-schooler while squidging balls of playdough for their toddler, but in my household it usually ends in tears. The toddler starts to eat the playdough, or lob it at the spaceship, or the pre-schooler decides she must have the lime-green dough for her spaceship furniture, right now, and she doesn't care if it's the very bit the toddler has just picked up a second before. Even doing things that both children enjoy can be harder than it sounds: swimming, painting, walks – all these activities will prove more satisfying for everyone concerned once everyone concerned is aged four years or over.

Children need to be loved and protected, and they also need to learn how to co-operate and comply with other people. Parents are primarily the ones who must teach them this. But it is not always so easy. Especially not on those days when you can't seem to get out of the house, nor get on

Tea for Three: The First Year

Children adjust to becoming and being a sibling gradually, and most will 'act out' their more negative feelings of jealousy, insecurity and anger in different ways at different stages. Since children come with an assortment of temperaments and also develop at very different rates, there can be no hard-and-fast rules about these stages, but broadly speaking, you can expect the following:

- First few days: reactions aimed at adults: deliberate naughtiness, regressing.
- One to four months: expressions of anxiety: fussing, becoming withdrawn, night-time waking, setbacks in toilet training, irrational fears and phobias.
- Four to eight months: reactions to sibling: jealousy, pinching, snatching, hitting.
- Eight months on: increasing conflict between children, greater and greater demands on parents.

The following reactions to a new baby's arrival are all well within the range of normal behaviour, and are likely to crop up during the first year.

- Ambivalence towards the baby: veering from friendly to hostile.
- Regressing: reverting to night-waking, thumbsucking, bedwetting and so on.
- Clingy behaviour: insecure of you, anxious about separations.
- Concern over losing things; panicking about minor setbacks.
- Irrational fears of the dark, of monsters, of water and so on.
- Jealousy and aggression.
- Faddiness with food.
- Deliberate naughtiness.
- Confrontations over rules and routines.
- Fussing, whining, being generally awkward.
- Baby talk, pretend crying, wanting a bottle/dummy/nappy.

Most of these reactions will sort themselves out within a few months. If after 12 months your older child is behaving aggressively towards you, displaying anxiety, or suffering from recurrent fears or phobias, you should seek professional advice.

NB: An increase in conflict between your children at the end of one year is entirely normal!

inside it; when the children veer from one flare-up to the next; when one seems intent on antagonising the other, and no one settles to anything long enough for you even to put the kettle on, let alone make a cup of desperately needed tea. The average toddler or pre-schooler has a great deal more time, energy and determination than the average exhausted mother-of-two. Children often win battles of will simply because they can stick it out longer. Children, as we all know, are adept at driving their parents to the very brink of their self-control, and then gently, ruthlessly, nudging them over the edge.

As the younger child leaves baby- and toddler-hood behind, the feeling of being overwhelmed that so many mothers experience at one time or another begins to drop off. Mothers who stay at home with their children, or who work part-time when they are very young, are the most likely to feel this 'lightening'. 'When my younger child was two, I suddenly felt myself emerging,' one mother said to me. 'You begin to see the light at the end of the tunnel around the time of their second birthday,' said another. This reflects both the child's growing physical independence, and also their increasing attachment to and need for people other than yourself. The intense involvement of the early months is changing and usually that brings more space for you to think your own thoughts, pursue your own interests, meet your own needs.

Life with two children at times resembles nothing so much as a vigorous game of squash in which you are the little black ball. At times even the most accomplished parents can forget everything they ever learned, or thought they knew, about child-rearing. When there are two children going full-tilt at you, and at each other, especially when you've been up three times in the night with one and up since six with the other, it becomes far harder to find time or space to work out what's going wrong, let alone work out what to do about it. Situations spiral rapidly out of control. Tempers flare with terrifying speed and ferocity. Attitudes may need reviewing, behaviour modifying, and changes implementing – but who's got the time or energy? With two small children rampaging through your life like Thing One and Thing Two, you're doing well to get yourself dressed in the morning, and undressed again at night, never mind the children, and who cares if you forgot to brush your teeth or comb your hair in between?

But no phase with children lasts forever. Knowing this is the great bonus in the pocket of the second-time parent; more than any other bit of information we may have gleaned from having our first child, this is the one that sees us through the darker days. With our second child we know that they won't always want to spend all day attached to the nipple; we know they won't go on waking at night forever; we know that the phase when they won't get dressed in the morning and won't get undressed at night is just that: a phase.

Give yourself time to adjust and adapt; give your children time to adjust and adapt. Be patient with yourself and with them. Above all, be realistic. The standards you maintained relatively easily with one child may be completely impossible with two. Accept the changes that come with your second child. Accept that things will shake down into some kind of pattern eventually, that things will get easier, that the first two years are undoubtedly the hardest, and, repeat it, that, even if it feels like it at times, this phase – like every other phase – won't last forever.

'I was just going to use the yellow!'

Five

SIBLINGS,
RIVALS & FRIENDS

A year or two into life with two children and you will almost certainly be well acquainted with at least some of the following statements:

'You like her better than me!'

'Yes, but who do you love *best*?'

'How come he gets two stories and I only get one?'

'You always stick up for her!'

'It's not fair!'

'He always gets more than me.'

'I *hate* having a little sister/brother.'

As we've already seen, from the moment our second child is born, we are caught up with not only managing the relationship with each of our children, but managing the relationship *between* them. As the weeks turn into months and the months into years, it is this relationship – the one between our children – that will take up more and more of our time, energy and ingenuity.

Siblings under the age of five average four conflicts an hour – one *every 15 minutes*! Even as children get older and the outright fights tail off, squabbling, rivalry, teasing and jealousy can continue unabated. Yet seeing our children being friends to one another is one of the greatest pleasures parenthood can bring. As Vicki Iovine puts it: 'Just when you think you can't take another step, out of the corner of your eye you will see the older child hug his new baby like he really means it, and you will weep and hear angels sing.'[1]

How our children get on together has a direct and profound impact on the quality of family life, as well as a significant long-term impact on how our children go on to make relationships in the future with people outside the family. As most of us know from our own lives, the relationship between siblings can reverberate in our lives long after we have left childhood behind us. 'Where you come in the family is *the* defining experience,' believes Natalie, mother of Benedict and Sebastian. 'I was the second girl, with a sister 18 months older and a brother three years younger. I'm sure that has had a huge influence on my life. My mother was always totally loving to all of us, but I knew her parents were disappointed when I wasn't a boy, so there was always this undercurrent of pressure to prove my worth. I felt I had to do everything just as well if not better than my sister. And then, to make matters worse, she had

Julian. It was this massive love affair. No one could compete. I had a very loving family, but there was always this feeling of being a little bit overlooked, squashed between this clever older sister and adored younger brother. Maybe that's why I became an actress: I'm still trying to get into that limelight!'

My older brother and I fought incessantly as children, but when I was 21 and he was 25 we decided to bury long years of differences and go on holiday together. My mother and grandmother were so aghast at the prospect that they rang each of us in turn to try and persuade us to change our minds. They were convinced it would be a complete disaster and one of us (at least) would return home in a body bag. We ignored them, booked a week's holiday in Crete and had a great time, with only one minor disagreement in seven days (about whose turn it was to go for the bread that morning – on such vast molehills are sibling quarrels often built). What I realised on further reflection was that their reactions to our decision to go on holiday together said a great deal about their feelings about their *own* siblings – my mother still has enormous difficulty holding a calm conversation with her younger sister, while my grandmother carried on referring to her older siblings as 'the ugly sisters' until she went to her grave, and long after they'd gone to theirs.

Patterns and expectations are set early within families and can be extraordinarily hard to change. If we can be imaginative, sensitive and thoughtful in the way we handle our children's relationships with one another, we give them the chance to develop the kind of relationship they want, not the one we consciously or unconsciously wish to impose upon them.

'When do they start playing together?' is one of the questions that new mothers-of-two are frequently heard asking their friends, relatives, neighbours and casual aquaintances. Before we have two children we envisage an endless vista of compatibility: in our fertile imaginations our little darlings spend happy hours together, building Lego towers, holding picnics for their teddies, making dens behind the sofa. Our children, we fondly assume, will be each other's playmates. And it's true, they will be – *eventually*. But in the first year or two after your second child is born the only game they'll play on a truly regular basis is an infant version of badminton with you as the shuttlecock.

Siblings are unlikely to play together reliably – or at least reliably peaceably – until the youngest one is nearer to three than two, and even then other factors such as personality, gender and age gap may still get in the way. Once the older child has cottoned on to the younger child's slave potential, you'll find you have time for the odd cup of coffee; if your children are particularly considerate/malleable/cowed, you may even get to read the paper from time to time.

Any parent who is also a sibling will have a stash of childhood memories of sibling misdemeanours perpetrated by them or at their expense. A friend of mine recalls spending one entire Sunday afternoon hiding in the laundry basket on the instructions of her four older siblings who'd told her they were playing hide-and-seek, but were actually exhibiting a common form of sibling humour. My own big brother's idea of fun was playing darts with a picture of me as the bull's-eye. Another time he mixed up a concoction of marmite, sugar, tomato ketchup and pepper, and persuaded me it was instant coffee – a drink I'd never tasted, but longed to since it was what he and his friends drank in the mysterious sanctum of his bedroom; as I sipped away, making appreciative noises, he rolled around in fits of mirth. I was no paragon myself and still squirm to recall some of the less kind things I did to my younger siblings when they were little and I was old enough to know better. There are other memories too, of course: superb day-long games of cowboys and Indians; life-threatening sleeping-bag races down the stairs; putting on plays in the cellar; making dens in the garden. Being a sibling certainly wasn't all bad, and yet I still wonder what lay behind those unremarkable, routine episodes of cruelty? Resentment, envy, boredom, dislike? It is hard to say, even now, but they remain sharply defined, significant, against the soft-focus backdrop of sweeter memories.

Once we become parents ourselves, we put our own childhood experiences firmly behind us, or think we do. We tell ourselves that our children will be good friends; we believe they will like – and love – each other; we hope they will understand and help each other. But sometimes, despite our plans, our children seem determined to be worst enemies. Sometimes, to our dismay, the only emotions a sibling seems to inspire are indifference, anger and loathing.

Coping with Jealousy

Far and away the biggest obstacle to friendship between siblings is jealousy. In the early weeks and months this is triggered – understandably enough – by the trials of having to share. Having a good relationship with your first-born before the second baby arrives is no insurance against jealousy; in fact, the more intense the involvement between you and your first-born, the more likely it is that you will have to cope with distress and jealousy after your second child is born.

Bringing home a new baby has been compared to your partner bringing home a new wife: from the older child's point of view, it's no great shakes. Suddenly, your parents, your toys, your high chair, your cot, even your clothes are up for grabs. As we saw in the last chapter, some instances of jealousy are par for the course. Shaking the cot, making a lot of noise when the baby has just dropped off to sleep, squeezing, taking the baby's dummy: these kinds of actions express a mixture of curiosity and jealousy. However exasperating for you, this kind of behaviour should not be taken too seriously; in fact, coming down too hard on a disoriented first-born at this stage can make for more trouble in the long run.

That said, the ferocity with which an older child can react to the arrival of a younger sibling can take parents by surprise, as Deborah, mother of Zoe and Caitlin, discovered: 'It was fine when Zoe first saw Caitlin at the hospital, but once she realised the baby was coming home and was going to live with us, she changed her mind. She was terribly jealous. She wanted me to do everything for her – push the pushchair, feed her, dress her, cuddle her. She had a lot of tantrums. It was all about this intruder coming between her and me and I completely understood how she felt and just tried to be as understanding and loving as possible. I tried to reassure her, tried to pour love and reassurance into her. It was very, very hard though, and we just had to ride it out.'

There are two very different schools of thought on how best to foster a good relationship between siblings in these early stages. The first school believes that the best approach, and the one most likely to minimise jealousy, is to keep the baby out of the picture from the word go; not to let the baby invade and disrupt the older child's world; not to flaunt your affection for the baby. In other words, advocates of this approach advise parents to avoid giving their older child any grounds for feeling jealous. The second school of thought, however, advocates the exact opposite, advising parents to bring the baby into the child's life as much as possible from the very beginning; letting the older child help with the baby; talking to the older child about the baby. The advice to parents is to encourage the first-born, from the outset, to feel *involved* with the baby, rather than *in competition* with it.

Research firmly suggests that the second approach is more likely to foster warm sibling relations in the long run.

Children take their cues from the adults around them: if you don't seem to think the baby is worth much, why should they? If you can leave the baby to scream, why should they care when their younger sibling gets upset? If, on the other hand, your older child sees you being affectionate and responsive to the baby, he or she will register that this is the right way to behave – even if he or she doesn't always manage it. The way your first-born reacts to the baby in the first few days is not an indication of how they will get on later, but the way *you* behave towards your children, and the way you handle the relationship between them is crucial.

From the outset, what you do with your children can create an environment in which jealousy and competitiveness thrive, or one in which conflicts can be resolved before they become personalised or ingrained. Your first-born needs to feel happy and secure in the new role of older sibling. He needs to have occasional perks and privileges; he needs to be protected from the baby (especially once it is crawling); he needs regular, uninterrupted time alone with you. Your first-born also needs to know that you understand and can bear his more negative feelings: he needs space and time to be sad, angry and confused about the changes in his life. He needs routines and guidelines, clear rules and boundaries, and lots of physical affection and positive attention.

The overriding principle is to encourage your children right from the start to see each other as separate individuals with differing needs and interests and temperaments – and to help them both to respect and tolerate those differences. Studies have found that in families where parents talk about the baby as a person right from the start, and involve the older child in discussions about the baby, the siblings had the closest relationship. Difficult as it will undoubtedly be at times, an openly loving approach to both children from the start is the best way to foster a good relationship between them in the long run.

As the baby gets more active and more intrusive, the raw, green-eyed jealousy that older children often feel in the first few weeks is usually displaced into territorial disputes over toys, games, books and, of course, your attention. 'Mine!' is the word that rings in the ears of many parents of small children. Jealousy quickly ceases to be a top-down affair: your younger child can feel jealous of your older one and may be increasingly adept at diverting attention back to himself when he wants it. In one of her studies of siblings, Judy Dunn observed a little girl called Polly, 'a particularly charming two-year-old', who became increasingly subtle and effective at getting her mother's attention away from her older sister as the weeks passed. 'When any games began between Joanne and her parents, she tried to intervene to draw attention to herself. Her efforts became more sophisticated month by month. At 24 months, when her mom was joining Joanne in playing a pretend game in which Joanne took her dolls to school, Polly simply charged into the conversation, insistently ordering her mom to "Look at my doll!" By two and a half her interventions became more subtle. One day she managed to join in the pretend game of shopping that Joanne and her mom were playing by cleverly deflecting the game to go her way. "My shop's got bananas for you! Come get my bananas!" Rather than reprimand Polly for interfering or gently persuade her to enter into Joanne's game, their mother turned her attention to buying Polly's bananas. Joanne was understandably upset.'[2]

Toddlers can be downright provocative towards older siblings and parents – and clearly enjoy the reactions they get. Natalie's younger son Sebastian, who is 20 months old, has recently discovered the thrill of the 'wind up': 'He's not at all naughty normally, but he really seems to delight in annoying Benedict at the moment. When he's watching television, he goes and stands right in front of the screen so that Ned can't see. Or he'll actually turn the television off. It drives Ned mad. And I can't say I blame him. If I take Sebastian away and try to engage him in some other activity, he just waits until I've gone and then does it again. It's incredibly deliberate.'

The relationship between siblings is not static. As children themselves change, so does the relationship between them. As the second child grows from a baby into a pre-schooler, there is a huge development in their social and intellectual abilities, and this in turn brings enormous changes

Ten Steps to Sibling Harmony

The seeds of friendship between siblings are sown from the moment your second child arrives on the scene.

● Show your children how to play together, starting with games of peekaboo and funny faces, and progressing over the months to tea parties and (gentle) ball games.

● Show your older child how much the little one likes her, watches her, smiles at her, quietens down for her, looks forward to seeing her.

● Encourage your children to communicate with each other. Ask your older one to 'interpret' for you – 'What do you think she's trying to say to us?' – and point out ways in which the baby is responding: 'He likes it when you sing to him'; 'See how she's listening when you talk to her?'

● Encourage identification by telling your older child all the things that he or she did at the same age, or by showing him pictures or videos of himself at same age.

● Encourage empathy and consideration by talking about the baby's needs and feelings: 'Do you think the baby might be a bit hot? Shall we take her hat off for a while?', 'Do you think the baby likes it when we rock him like this?', 'I don't think she likes having a dirty nappy, what do you think?'

● Once the baby starts to crawl, help your older child to find solutions to the problem of a mobile, inquisitive younger sibling, for example by moving 'special' things out of the baby's reach.

to their relationship with their older brother or sister. But the changes are not always what you might expect. Judy Dunn observed 100 children in 50 families over a period of 18 months, and found that there was no change in how much children interacted with one another from when the second child was 18 months old to when he or she was 36 months. The amount of time playing and fighting *remained the same*.[3] What changed radically, however, was the nature of the interaction between the children as the younger child took an increasingly active part in initiating both playing and fighting. First-born children often find themselves having to rethink their approach to a younger sibling at this stage to take account of an altogether more assertive presence, someone who can now join in games, but who is equally able to spoil them.

Parents like to see their children enjoying each other's company (perhaps because it makes them feel better about imposing a sibling on their unsuspecting first-born in the first place!), but they consistently *overestimate* how well their children are getting on. Robert Stewart found that one year after the birth of the second child, 75 per cent of mothers reported co-operation and sharing between their children, while only 12 per cent made any mention of infant intrusion or aggression. When researchers asked the first-born children in these families how they were getting on with their younger siblings, they painted a less rosy picture: at eight months, 50 per cent of first children reported aggression or intrusions by their younger sibling. By 12 months, this had risen to 85 per cent.[4] That's an awful lot of disgruntled children.

Clearly, being a sibling is a far more stressful business than we like to admit. Very rarely, though, do parents make enough allowance for just how stressful. As the younger one gets not just more mobile, but more capable of interfering, provoking and annoying his or her older sibling, the relationship between them becomes more conflictive, more charged, not less so. Most books on childcare, if they mention the subject at all, tend to suggest strategies for the first few months; very few take adequate account of how the relationship between siblings develops over time. Nor do they mention that, as the relationship between siblings changes, you may need to change too. In the early weeks and months, it helps to spend time with both children, rather than keep them separate, because this fosters a sense of involvement and connection between the children. As they get older, however, you need to adapt your approach to their relationship to take account of their changing needs, personalities and abilities.

Janice, mother of Gareth and Eva, describes how this happened with her children. 'Eva is a real extrovert and likes to be at the centre of things, and preferably at the centre of everyone's attention too! When she was a baby it didn't affect Gareth that much, but it definitely changed as she got older. She always wanted to do whatever he was doing, and it was very hard for him. If Gareth was playing the piano, she wanted to. If Gareth was drawing, she wanted to draw. If Gareth was playing snap or something, Eva wanted to. Because she's also a very determined character, it wasn't that easy to divert her into something else, and if she didn't get her own way, she'd throw a tantrum, really scream the house down. We didn't really notice, but gradually Gareth became quite withdrawn and morose. I think he was actually a bit depressed. We were still thinking of Eva as this little bundle of fun, whereas in fact she was being a bit of a bully to him. When she tried to join in with him, I tended to see it as a good thing, sort of the beginning of them becoming friends. I don't know why, but I just didn't see that he wasn't enjoying it all. He needed time off from Eva, not time with her. And he needed much more protection from her than we were giving him. Once we finally realised what was going on, we sat down with Gareth and talked about it, and all this resentment just poured out, how she always got her own way, how she ruined everything, how much he hated her! After that, we started taking a much firmer line with her, making it clear that it was not OK for her to barge in on whatever he was doing. I made more effort to get her doing her own activities so that she wouldn't bother him. Gareth got better at saying no to her too. Nowadays they get on incredibly well; they're always off playing games together. It's just wonderful. I love seeing them together like that. They have a really great relationship.'

As children get older, their friendship grows, and so do the occasions for jealousy. 'Why can't I come too?' wails the younger one, as you and your first-born head off for a scintillating visit to the supermarket. 'I don't want to go to school,' moans your older one as your toddler smugly waves her off with one hand while keeping a proprietorial grip of your left leg with the other. Whatever an objective cost-benefit analysis of any situation might reveal, from the viewpoint of siblings, the other one's grass looks greener. When your younger child gets his first new item of clothing in two years, for your first-born it's as if all those hand-me-downs had never been: 'I want new gloves too,' she complains. 'You've got new gloves,' you gently remind her. 'No! I want new gloves like *his*.'

However often you explain the reverse, older children keenly perceive the advantages of being a younger sibling, not to mention the disadvantages of being a sibling at all. 'If you hadn't had S.,' my daughter announced recently, 'you wouldn't have two children. And if you didn't have two children, you wouldn't be writing a book about it, and then you wouldn't have to work so much, and then you'd have more time to spend with *me*.' Conclusion: it's all *his* fault! There was a certain impeccable logic to her reasoning that she was neglected because of the presence of her younger brother, but of course it was I who was 'to blame' for his birth; I who had found having two children an eye-opening experience; I who had decided to write about it.

Children are extraordinarily forgiving of their parent's foibles and failings, but as my daughter demonstrated, that doesn't solve the problem of what to do with their feelings of anger or sadness. From a child's point of view, directing their uncomfortable emotions at a younger sibling is often the obvious solution. As parents, we may have to listen quite carefully to hear what our children are really telling us. Rebuking a child for feeling resentful of a sibling is a waste of time if the resentment is really aimed not at the sibling but at a parent.

Sibling rivalry cuts both ways, of course. As the older one advances into the world beyond the home, the younger one can feel acutely conscious of all the perks of seniority: having friends to play; learning to ride a bike without stabilisers; trips to the cinema. There isn't one younger sibling on this planet who has not had at some time in their childhood a woeful moment of realisation that they will *never ever* get to be the same age at the same time as their older sibling – a fact that older siblings, surprise surprise, grasp with astonishing speed!

Jealousy between siblings stems from children's growing awareness of their differences. That awareness is then fed and watered on a daily basis by their innate talent for detecting unequal treatment, or more devastating still, parental preference. The phrase 'it's not fair' seems to enter most children's vocabulary when they are about four years old. Sometimes your children are right; it's not fair, and you need to think about what they are trying to tell you. Responding with the words, 'Life's not fair', is hardly helpful.

Managing Anger and Fighting

As well as avoiding situations that cause conflict, you also need to identify the feelings that provoke it. This applies to six-year-olds as much as two-year-olds. Jeremy is talking to me about his younger brother Jack: 'It's really hard being the oldest. The younger one gets all the attention. It's not fair, 'cos he gets carried more than I do.' Jeremy clearly feels aggrieved about the preferential treatment he thinks his little brother gets. Are there any good things about being the older child, I ask him. Without hesitation, Jeremy grins: 'Yeah, I can beat him up!'

Jeremy's parents are intelligent, gentle people, but like many parents, particularly the parents of sons, they take the view that 'all children fight from time to time', and have adopted a 'hands-off' strategy to their boys' conflict. The idea that boys want and need to fight is often used as a convenient excuse by parents who don't know what to do about conflict between their children. As a result many brothers put up with years of physical bullying that their parents would protect them from if they were girls. In Jeremy's case, he has certain grounds for resentment. His younger brother has health problems, which means that he does indeed get preferential treatment from time to time. If Jeremy's parents could allow him to express his jealousy in other ways, his younger brother might not have to bear the brunt of it. Instead, Jack has quickly learnt how to turn his weakness into a strength, and exploits his 'invalid' status for all he's worth. Cuddled up in his dad's arms or on his mum's lap, or tucked up in bed, is the safest place to be. Perhaps not surprisingly, Jack suffers from an assortment of undefined symptoms, although there is nothing obviously or officially wrong with him.

Fighting and aggression, if left untended, can become real problems. Parents are far more keen to see their children getting on than to acknowledge that they aren't. Even today my mother-in-law insists that her two boys got on fine as children. 'Oh they fought a bit when they were very little, but really they got on terribly well most of the time.' This is not how either of her adult sons remembers their childhood. One feels shame and bafflement about the way he behaved towards his younger sibling, while the other thinks the constant physical and verbal attacks he endured have affected him deeply. As adults, they have at last been able to talk openly and frankly about their childhood and have forged a close adult relationship.

It doesn't always follow that children fight because they don't get on. Frequent arguments between young children are not necessarily a sign of a bad relationship, or even of negative feelings: 'Siblings who quarrel a lot and are very competitive are often quite friendly and co-operative in other ways', according to Judy Dunn.[5] From the parent's point of view, children's fights can look pretty similar: one child is shrieking its head off, the other is in a corner looking sullen and rebellious; invariably we round on the quieter child with a resounding, 'What have you done? What happened?' We base our conclusions on the last 'incident' and, often wrongly, assume this latest fight is a straight repeat. But children fight for numerous reasons: maybe because they feel jealous, maybe because they're upset or angry about something, maybe because their personalities clash, or because there's a genuine conflict of interest over an issue or object. If we can help them to work out what is causing the conflict at any particular moment, rather than assume that fights always break out for the same reason, we can help them to respond appropriately, as well as responding appropriately ourselves.

Easier said than done, of course. For many of us, handling the feelings of anger, panic and sheer desperation that warring children rouse in us is at least as difficult as handling the anger they rouse in each other. Ruth remembers finding this a great problem for a while with her two daughters, Hannah and Rachel. 'When Hannah was about three and Rachel was about nine months, Hannah went through a phase of being terribly jealous. I couldn't leave them alone together for a moment. As soon as I wasn't looking, she'd push Rachel over or pinch her. One time I came back just in time to see her about to hit Rachel with a cricket bat. It was quite deliberate, and Hannah definitely knew what she was doing. She could be really vicious, and it was horrible seeing my own child behave in this way. I found it very hard to be understanding. You're meant to stay calm, aren't you, but often I was so furious with her for hurting Rachel that I'd be yelling at her or picking her up too roughly before I'd even had time to think. It was an instinctive reaction, to protect the baby, but it was frightening to feel so angry, so out of control myself.'

As children get older, their capacity for arguing over seemingly nothing, and their willingness to resort to bashing each other over the head, becomes more and more exasperating. As parents we need to think about our own experiences as children and the kind of role models we were brought up with. We may need to remind ourselves how it felt to be on the receiving end of our parent's anger, how it felt being hit, or severely punished in some way.

Peter Eldrid, head of training at Parentline Plus, thinks that acknowledging how you're feeling is an important first step. 'We try and help parents to identify when things regularly go wrong. Mealtimes, bedtimes, getting ready for school are all very stressful times of day in families. We ask them if there are particular behaviours or particular settings that drive them to breaking point. Being able to recognise when you reach that point makes it easier to step out of the situation rather than being dragged down by it.'

For the parent at breaking point, what may be needed are immediate alternatives to physical violence, such as counting to ten, punching a table, taking a deep breath, or going into another room. 'It's also important to look at what happens when things go well,' says Eldrid, 'to think about what things make a positive difference.'

Ruth worked out that Hannah was most likely to hurt Rachel when she was on the phone. Other parents have described how their children always seem to start fighting when they're cooking, or talking to other adults. If you can identify the trigger, as Eldrid says, you can often find ways of anticipating the situation or avoiding it altogether: Ruth started taking the baby with her when she answered the phone; another mother kept a tube of Smarties by the cooker, and rewarded the children with three Smarties each if they let her cook tea in peace. Another strategy is to explain in advance what is going to happen, how you want them to behave, and how you will reward them afterwards. This is otherwise known as the 'Art of Suggestion', to which even very small human beings are surprisingly susceptible. Announce in a calm clear voice, 'I am now going to cook tea/answer the phone/go to the loo. I'd like you to play quietly with the Lego/Barbie/toy cars until I've finished. When I come back, I'm going to read you each a story.'

Sometimes the best solution to sibling fights is to change tack completely. My normally pacific daughter would invariably pick fights with her little brother at bath-time. She would hog all the bath toys and then kick him if he tried to get any for himself. Bath-times quickly deteriorated into screaming matches, until we eventually twigged that sharing a bath was a share too far. She needed that particular space to herself.

In some cases the younger child will be the aggressor, and when this happens it is important that the older child isn't made to feel responsible. Caroline, mother of Tom and Bridget, recalls how for several months Tom's face was covered in livid scratches that had been inflicted by his two-year-old sister. 'It was very distressing. Tom is a very gentle child and

Helping Children to Handle Conflict

- Be consistent, calm and very firm about violence and aggression.
- Have a 'no hitting' rule, and make sure everyone sticks to it, including parents.
- Avoid rewarding aggressive behaviour with lots of attention. If you make a great fuss, for example by issuing lengthy lectures or insisting on 'a proper apology', it will be harder for your child to understand whether she has done something bad (since Mummy is cross) or good (since Mummy is being very attentive).
- Avoid making a joke of aggression. Telling off your child for hitting a sibling, or another child, and then, in his hearing, joking about what a 'little hooligan' he's turning into can only confuse him as to what you really expect of him.
- Never ignore physical violence. Separate children who are hurting each other, or in danger of hurting each other; immediately remove toys that are being used as weapons.
- Acknowledge how both children are feeling, not just the one who has been hurt. This encourages the aggressor to think about how it feels to be on the receiving end of his or her treatment.
- With very young children, avoid situations which tend to lead to flare-ups.
- Older children can be helped to find alternative strategies to hitting: 'When she starts to ruin your game, ask her to stop.' 'If he doesn't stop, call me straight away.' 'If she takes the toy you are playing with, try offering her something to swap with.'
- Help older children to pre-empt fights altogether, by talking about both the causes of conflict and the feelings they arouse. 'If he hits you again, what could you do apart from hitting back?' 'Why do you think she reacted like that this morning?' 'If he snatches the toy you're playing with, try offering him something to swap with.'
- Suggest and try out alternative targets for violent feelings – cushions, drawings, football.
- Encourage children to use words not actions to express anger. As soon as children can talk, you can start to help them to put their feelings into words.
- Acknowledge and accept that your children will have negative feelings towards each other at times. Telling a child to stop being angry with a sibling who has just wrecked the game he was playing is pointless. Telling him, simply, that you can see how angry he is often defuses the situation with dramatic speed.

would never hit anyone, but Bridget went through a phase of just lashing out at him, completely unprovoked, leaving these awful bleeding gashes. I'd tell her off and make her apologise, but she didn't seem to care. I think she enjoyed the reaction she got.' Caroline dealt with the problem by helping Tom to recognise situations in which Bridget was likely to scratch him, but she was careful not to make him feel that her attacks were his fault. 'Maybe it was a way of getting his attention, because as she got older and could join in his games, she gradually grew out of it.'

Sibling conflict is as old as Cain and Abel and it's a foolish parent who thinks it possible to have children and not encounter any symptoms of rivalry somewhere along the line. With our first child, we get a hint of what lies ahead when our baby tries to commandeer the toy that someone else's baby is currently playing with. But these low-key encounters are as nothing to what we have to deal with between our own beloved progeny. It's the difference between watching a rugby scrum on TV and being the ball.

We can't shrug off our involvement in our children's skirmishes. We're there in the stadium whether we like it or not. But whether we choose to be rugby ball, team coach, umpire or on-looker in relation to their conflicts will have a marked effect on how their relationship with one another, and with us, develops over time.

The Rugby Ball Parent (and there are days when we are all Rugby Ball Parents) tends to ignite conflict by getting too involved, and prolong conflict by staying too involved. These parents find it hard to bear their children quarrelling. Perhaps they come from families in which anger and disagreements were frowned upon. Perhaps they have unrealistic expectations about how siblings should behave. Rugby Ball Parents worry that somehow they are to blame for their children's discord, and therefore feel they are responsible for smoothing the waters. Rugby Ball Parents are entirely well intentioned, but they make it very difficult for children to have a relationship of their own, because they are always coming between them, trying to build bridges, but just as often putting up barriers. They provide their children with a foolproof strategy for getting their attention, since they usually rush in and stop fights without stopping to assess the situation first. My grandmother was a wonderful grandmother, but she was definitely a Rugby Ball Mother. Her daughters not only had to go through her to communicate with each other, they did the same thing to communicate with their father. Throughout their childhood, their relationship was full of frustration and misunderstanding, and having never learnt to communicate as children, their conversations even as adults often go awry. Rugby Ball Parents forget that real closeness between siblings is impossible if there's always an obstacle keeping them apart. Children who aren't allowed near each other, physically and emotionally, will never learn how to be close without fighting.

The On-Looker Parent, in complete contrast, adopts a non-interventionist approach to sibling quarrels. She takes the view that you can't fight other people's battles for them, and that children must learn to sort out their own conflicts. As a result, she often lets her children get *too* close. (On-Looker Parents, not surprisingly, are often the grown-up children of Rugby Ball Parents.) While it is true that nearly all children fight with their siblings at some time or other, On-Looker Parents are not helping their children – or the relationship between them – as much as they like to think. Parents who remain steadfastly neutral during their children's fights forget that children may not be ready to fight their own battles. For a start, they are not equal combatants. A three-year-old will have less self-control than a five-year-old; a ten-year-old can run faster and hit harder than a seven-year-old. A hands-off approach from parents can easily feel like abandonment to children, and can be crushing to a less confident child, while encouraging aggression in a more assertive or stronger one. On-Looker Parents tend to ignore the fact that children need help and protection and guidance in sorting out differences; they need caring adults to teach them negotiation skills before they can begin to handle conflict effectively themselves.

Next up for consideration is the Umpire Parent, who sometimes stands on the sidelines and sometimes gets into the middle of the fray. Wherever she is, she'll be trying to be fair at all costs. The trouble is, strictly fair solutions can be anything but. Confiscating a toy that one child wants and the other child has just snatched is 'fair' to both children, in that neither now has what they want, but it is hardly a satisfactory solution to the problem. Judging a situation on its appearance alone just exacerbates children's feelings of resentment and hostility – towards each other and towards you. Conflict is a product of strong feelings, and children need help dealing with those feelings and not just with the conflict. If we stop children fighting without ever finding out why they're fighting, we won't make much progress and neither will they. The Umpire Parent is a good law-enforcer, but often overlooks the importance of helping children to understand the emotions that give rise to the conflict and arise out of it, or of teaching them to think of more constructive ways of dealing with those feelings. Siblings do need umpires at times, but in conjunction with a good coach.

There are good coaches and bad coaches, of course, and this applies to the Team Coach Parent. A bad coach tends to side with one child (usually the younger one) over the other, and quickly undermines the confidence of the other team by never letting play take place on a level playing field. The bad Team Coach Parent is unable to see that the baby/toddler/pre-schooler is not so vulnerable as all that, and may in fact be committing most of the fouls. Favouritism always fuels resentment, which in turn increases the likelihood of conflict. When parents take sides, particularly if they persistently side with one child against the other, they do untold damage to the relationship between their children. Even very young children are acutely aware of and upset by this kind of favouritism.

The good Team Coach Parent, on the other hand, will build up both teams, working with the strengths and weaknesses of each, bringing out the best in both. The good parent coach will show a hot-tempered child how to express anger and frustration without hitting, or help a timid child to find ways of asserting herself, or discuss with an older child how he might protect space and possessions from an encroaching younger sibling. Good coaches nurture the ability of both children to resolve conflicts without hurting, and to tolerate differences without resentment; they help children to think about the causes of conflict, the underlying emotions that lead to fighting, while also giving them ideas and strategies for handling conflict when it occurs. The child who has been well coached will feel supported by his parent, but not helpless without her. When siblings receive the help they need to deal with the scratchier aspects of siblinghood, they can face each other fearlessly, communicate with each other openly, and with time develop the kind of relationship every parent dreams of for her children.

Problem-solving

The following technique for problem-solving requires you to be part-umpire and part-team coach and enables children to resolve conflicts by themselves, while at the same providing time them with the parental support and involvment they may still need. This helps children to develop confidence in their ability to sort out problems between themselves.

• Summarise the situation in non-judgemental terms: 'There's one tennis racket and two children wanting to use it.' 'You both want to tell me something, but I can only listen to one person at a time.'

• State each child's position, taking care not to label behaviour as good or bad. 'John, you want the next go with the racket, and Jane, you think your turn isn't over yet.' 'Kate, you have something quick you want to say. Harry, you want to tell me something very important that happened to you today.'

• Express your confidence in their ability to reach a solution by themselves. Depending on their age you can leave the solution entirely up to them, or gently · guide them in the right direction. Older children will be fine with, 'I'm sure you can work it out between you.' Younger children will need a little more guidance: 'You need to agree whose go it is, and how long each go will last. I'm sure you can sort it out between you. Let me know when you've decided.'

• Leave the room, or go a little distance away, but stay within hearing distance.

• If tempers flare up again, go through the steps again, slowly and clearly. Focus attention on how each child is feeling, rather than on the conflict itself. 'John, you look very worried.' 'Jane, I can see you're feeling very angry.'

• When they succeed in resolving the problem, praise them to the skies, tell them how well they handled the situation and how pleased you are.

(Adapted from *Siblings Without Rivalry* by Adele Faber and Elaine Mazlish.)

When parents intervene in quarrels in appropriate ways, they are – at least in theory – taking the opportunity to teach their children about patience, tolerance, consideration, rights, responsibilities. Obviously clumsy, angry or unjust interventions on the side of one sibling against another can set up resentment, bitterness and anger. At its best, however, a well-timed, carefully handled intervention is part of the process of moral education that all children need if they are to manage conflict confidently later in life. As Steve Biddulph puts it in *The Secret of Happy Children*, 'Whenever we intervene with children, our aim should be to help them learn what will work and serve them well as adults.'[6] Biddulph's view is that this comes down to striking a balance. 'A person who is being mistreated in some way needs to be able to say so out loud, with conviction, and to do so early on (before they feel or act violent). Anger and violence are not the same thing. Violence is anger gone wrong. An adult learns to moderate their anger so that it has impact, but does not do damage or become abusive. If our child shows too little anger, they may be seen as a wimp, and be pushed around or used by other kids. Too much anger makes them unpopular or even a bully. Getting this balance right is what our kids need to learn about.'[7]

Handled sensitively, sibling rivalry can be a passing phase; handled badly, it can become a lifelong condition. A 20-year-old I know is still simmering with resentment and hurt because her parents always told her it was her fault when she and her younger brother fought as children. 'They used to tell me to share more, to be more patient, to be more understanding. It was never, ever him who was in the wrong, always me.' This young woman and her brother still both live at home with their parents; the only time they talk is when one of them answers the phone and it is for the other.

Sometimes conflict between siblings serves as a coded message that parents may not much want to hear. Children are sensitive emotional barometers and pick up on the stresses around them. In families where parents are overly preoccupied with their own problems, or where there is a high level of marital discord, children can feel ignored or overlooked, and fighting with a sibling may be the most effective way to express anger and resentment, and the only way to get parents' attention. This is also true of families in which one parent is emotionally or physically absent, or there are major unresolved conflicts between parents.

Siblings in Step-families

For the substantial number of children born into step-families each year, all the normal problems associated with siblings are magnified. Step-families now account for more than eight per cent of all families with dependent children, and around 40,000 children under five now live in families of divorced couples. An estimated 28 per cent of children will experience the divorce of their parents before they reach the age of 16. A large number of these divorced parents go on to marry again (currently, around two in every five marriages are remarriages), taking their children with them into new families. Eighty-four per cent of step-families have at least one child from the mother's previous relationship, 12 per cent have a child from the man's previous relationship, and four per cent of step-families have children from both partners' previous relationships.[8]

Step-families have additional pressures to contend with, and for children of divorced parents, one of these pressures is having to negotiate often ambivalent relationships with step- or half-siblings, with whom they may share one or neither parent. Children are remarkably resilient and adaptable, but the emotional dynamics of life in a step-family are seldom straightforward, as Celia, mother of Benjamin and Frances, recalls from her own childhood. Three when her parents divorced and eight when her mother had another baby with her new husband, Celia is now raising her children on her own since the breakdown of her marriage.

'I remember when mum said she was having another baby being very pleased about the idea of having a little sister, but once Gemma was born I was just consumed with jealousy. There's a photo taken the day after, and everyone's smiling at the baby, and I'm sitting there with this thunderous look on my face, just miserable. My stepfather clearly preferred his own daughter to me, and was very strict with me while Gemma could do no wrong. My mother never stuck up for me. She just did whatever my stepfather wanted. I really hated my half-sister; I felt she'd ruined my life.' For a long time after she left home, Celia had no contact with her family, but eventually her younger sister got in touch, and they slowly began to disentangle the past. 'Gemma phoned me out of the blue one day and told me she was pregnant. We met up and started talking about when we were children. She told me that she'd always wanted me to like her, and had hated the way her father behaved. I slowly began to see that a lot of what I felt towards Gemma was actually resentment about my stepfather and anger at the way he treated me. Gemma and I are quite good friends these days! Both being mothers ourselves has helped.'

Robert, a language teacher in Gloucestershire, married his second wife, Janet, three years after his first wife died of breast cancer. He had a two-and-a-half-year-old son, Billy, by his first marriage, and when Billy was five, Robert and Janet had a little girl, Emily. As Robert recalls, it was the start of a very difficult time for the whole family. 'We had a lot of problems with Billy – he was terribly jealous of Janet at first and then transferred all of his anger on to the baby. Even before she was born, he would sometimes try to hit Janet's stomach, and afterwards he would try to hurt Emily when we weren't watching. He seemed to equate her birth with his mother's death; in his mind Emily was in some way to blame for Marion dying. It took all of our patience and understanding to keep reassuring Billy that I still loved him, that Janet wasn't going to die, and that Emily wasn't the enemy.'

The arrival of a half- or step-sibling can, of course, be an enriching, positive event in a child's life. A recent study of 50 children who'd grown up in step-families found that the birth of a half-sibling can forge a bond between the older child and the step-parent, as both are now linked by loving the new child. One of the children in this study described how the birth of a half-sister made her feel like they were 'a proper family' after all.[9] Relationships with siblings varied hugely and ranged from indifference to intense love or hatred, depending on a mixture of influences, but most of the children in the study felt close to their half-siblings and step-siblings. For some, step-siblings were undoubtedly a source of additional misery, but for others, step-siblings provided support at a stressful time in their lives. One of the women interviewed by Gill Gorell-Barnes and her colleagues in their book, *Growing Up in Step-families*, explained, 'We all got a little bit of strength from each other… I think we all helped each other through it.'[10]

If becoming a step-sibling coincides with the formation of a new and happier family unit, this greatly increases the chances of the ensuing relationship between the children also being a good one. Research shows that married parents who fight all the time are just as bad for children's well-being as parents who get divorced, and it is probably a good thing that the custom of 'staying together for the children's sake' has had its day. But from the children's point of view, leaping from the fire of one bad marriage into the frying pan of another is probably the worst scenario of all, and it is rare for siblings – whole, step- or half- – to enjoy a close relationship when the adults around them consistently model behaviour that shows them how *not* to get along.

That said, all families have their problems, their hidden or not-so-hidden tensions, and in most households conflict between children and between adults is not an indication of major difficulties, but just a common if regrettable aspect of family life. Hostility, rivalry and conflict occur for many reasons and are reinforced in many ways. Children, thankfully, are more open to suggestion than their parents tend to be, and in most cases, parents can make a huge difference to the level of sibling conflict simply by the way they handle it.

In their excellent book, *Siblings Without Rivalry*, Adele Faber and Elaine Mazlish explore in detail why children fight and how parents are often unwittingly responsible for creating the conditions in which conflict flourishes. They show how parents often compare their children without realising they are doing so, or stereotype them, casting them into roles that leave them little room for maneouvre, instead creating inflexible patterns of behaviour and response. They also explain why parental intervention is so often counter-productive, stopping the dispute perhaps, but without addressing the underlying causes of conflict.

Their top three commandments for parents of two or more children are: never compare, never accuse, never take sides. Instead, in Faber and Mazlish's words: 'Children should have the freedom to resolve their own differences. Children are also entitled to adult intervention when necessary. If one child is being abused by the other, either physically or verbally, we've got to step in. If there's a problem that's disrupting the entire household, we've got to step in. If there's a problem that keeps coming up that hasn't yielded to their solutions, we've got to step in. But here's the difference: we intervene, not for the purpose of settling their argument or making a judgment, but to open the blocked channels of communication so that they can go back to dealing with each other.'[11]

Parents are often advised to share out their attention as fairly and evenly as possible, but treating children fairly does not necessarily mean treating them the same. Children need to feel equal in our affections, equally loved and respected and valued, but they don't want to be treated like clones. Children don't want to feel the same as their siblings, they want to feel different and special.

And When to Do Nothing

However much we do to foster good sibling relations, some things about the way our children's relationship develops are out of our hands. For a start, the age gap will play a part in how they get along together. A bigger age gap will diminish the chances of your children being playmates. For Laura this is a regrettable result of having spaced her children four years apart: 'Sam will sometimes agree to play with Zak as a favour to me, but he's basically not very interested in him. Sam is nearly seven now and into action men and computer games and his own friends, and Zak is just too young. Sometimes Sam'll let Zak join in his games if he does as he's told, but he quickly loses patience if Zak starts messing it up. I hope they will like each other as they get older, but I don't really expect them to be good friends, not while they're children anyway – the age gap is just too big.'

If your children are closer in age, the likelihood of them becoming friends and playmates is greater, but there may be a bumpier path. Felicity, a full-time mother-of-three, is married to Dougal, a furniture-maker. Their two boys were born only 20 months apart. 'To begin with the older one was very jealous and quite violent towards his little brother. I had to watch them all the time, couldn't leave them for a second, which was completely exhausting. But by the time the little one was about 18 months that had changed totally, and they were beginning to play really well together. They liked doing the same kinds of things – kicking a ball about, pushing each other round on the tricycle. And their personalities also helped: the little one just worshipped his older brother and the older one is very kind-hearted, so gradually, despite his best intentions, his little brother won him round! Now they're five and seven and they're best mates.'

Age Gap and Sibling Harmony

Age gap is by no means the most important factor in ensuring sibling harmony. More significant than age gap are:

- The sex of the children.
- The temperament of the first child.
- The father's relationship with the first child, before and after the birth.
- How the parents prepared for and responded to the second child.

Gender also has marked effect on the likelihood of sibling rivalry and jealousy. Same-sex siblings have more conflicts, and first-born children with siblings of the same sex have more trouble adjusting. Boys are particularly likely to become withdrawn after the birth of a younger brother, and if not treated with sensitivity, may become angry and hostile later on. The flip-side of this is that same-sex siblings are also somewhat more likely to be very close. Children of different genders are less likely to fight so fiercely, but also less likely to become inseparable friends, at least in childhood.

Personality plays a definite role in how well your children will get along, and sometimes the fact is that they simply don't and won't. Charlotte is the mother of two daughters, now aged six and eight, but the signs of them becoming close friends are still distant. 'They just aren't very compatible. The younger one is gregarious and confident and thrives on attention, while the older one is much less sure of herself, quite shy and quiet. If it were the other way round, it might work better because Flora could protect her little sister, but as it is, Saskia doesn't need any protecting. She's always been more than able to stand her own ground. If anything it's Flora who needs the protection from her bossy little sister!'

In certain circumstances, the normal causes of insecurity, jealousy and resentment between siblings will be greatly exacerbated. When one child has special needs, as a result of a physical, emotional or psychological impairment or disability, the other will have a greater challenge than usual.

Sian and William run a small organic food business. Their second child Megan was born with a cleft palate, and needed a series of operations, which caused her parents a great deal of anxiety. 'Simon, our son, coped very well at the time,' recalls Sian. 'But afterwards he became very moody and unco-operative. He was fine with Megan but aggressive with me, hitting and kicking me and saying he hated me. Then he started refusing to go to school and wetting the bed at night and we realised there was a real problem. We'd assumed he was fine, but in fact he'd just bottled up all his feelings. Once the crisis with Megan was over, it all came out. When we sat down with Simon and talked it through, we were really shocked to realise that he'd thought all the fuss over Megan meant that we didn't love him any more.'

It is important to recognise that physical or mental disability puts strain not just on the parents but on other children in the family too, and that all

Golden Rules for Happy Siblings

- Don't assume your children will be best friends, or think you can make them be – it's their decision, not yours.
- Talk about the younger sibling as a person from the start.
- Treat your children as equals, but not as clones.
- Don't expect your older child to look after your younger child.
- Emphasise unique qualities, but avoid labels. Even positive labels are unhelpful: the 'clever', 'charming', 'funny' child can as easily feel oppressed and constrained by these labels as the 'clumsy', 'stupid', 'selfish' one.
- Describe specific behaviour instead of making generalised statements. 'You weren't watching where you were going' is more helpful than 'You're such a clumsy oaf.'
- Avoid stereotyping children. The one who's good at games may be desperate to sit down with a good book from time to time. The academic child may be longing to join a gym club.
- Encourage an attitude of mutual tolerance and generosity. This must be a two-way process: if the older child is always the one expected to make allowances for a younger sibling, he or she will inevitably begin to feel aggrieved. Make sure that the younger one makes space for the older one at times too. This can be done in small ways, for example by gently telling the one-year-old that he can't play with a certain toy, because it is a special toy and belongs to his big sister. The one-year-old may not understand, but the three-year-old will get the message loud and clear.

of you may well need help in coping. That said, there is no reason why siblings can't be loving and close even when one has a problem of some kind. Children with handicapped siblings are often impressively able to strike the balance between treating their brother or sister like anyone else and showing consideration for the ways in which they are different. These children are often the most fiercely protective and supportive of their sibling.

The arrival of a sibling is a landmark in a child's life. Siblings provide a child with his or her first taste of competitiveness, jealousy, rivalry, aggression, loss – but also companionship, co-operation, tolerance, patience and considerateness. Siblings provide the forum for all sorts of invaluable learning – if all goes well. How to negotiate, how to resolve conflict without verbal or physical violence, how to tolerate and even respect difference, how to compete, how to lose, how to empathise and reciprocate and share (as well as how to tolerate not sharing).

The second child alters the family environment and the dynamics of the relationships within that family. This can be the catalyst for latent problems to become manifest, or existing tensions to be resolved. This can be when the fault-lines in a family split wide open, when the skeletons come tumbling out of closets, or conversely when a family finds its feet and begins to feel more stable. How our children get on with one another reveals much about other aspects of family life: their relationship with their parents, their feelings of security and anxiety – children who fight all the time may be telling us something about problems or tensions elsewhere in the family. The relationship *between* our children says a lot about what we, their parents, bring to our relationship *with* our children – a preference for girls, for boys, for babies; about how we ourselves handle conflict, competition, jealousy and anger; even about the kinds of relationships we had with our own brothers and sisters.

For parents – we hapless mortals who bring these small creatures into being with such high hopes and gilded fantasies – seeing our children behaving unkindly or violently towards one another is extremely painful. The regularity with which we do so can dull the pain, but each episode of conflict is nevertheless an attack on us too, a strike at our idealism, our longing for untainted love. Perhaps this is why parents so often react with unreasonable anger when children fight: it is hard for us to bear the fact that these products of our love, these little vessels of our longings, have less-than-pure feelings and impulses towards each other. When we shout 'Stop shouting!' and yank the children apart with as much force as they've just used on each other, we feel demoralised and undermined. At that moment when the four-year-old has just brutally kicked the two-year-old, in response to the two-year-old savagely pulling out a handful of the four-year-old's hair, and in response to both, you are about to descend like a raging banshee on the pair of them, if at that precise moment we could stop time and scrutinise our own feelings, we would find, behind the rage, a confused amalgam of dismay, shame, fear and sadness.

Handling rivalry between our children requires us to dig deep into our reserves of intuition and patience and self-control; it requires us to hone our capacity for impartiality and self-control; above all, it requires us to be honest with ourselves about what we bring to the situation, to acknowledge what we might be doing to fuel the fires we so long to extinguish. Whatever strategies we devise to defend against the disappointment of realising that our children are not angels, that we have not perfected ourselves or the world by their presence, we are still their best hope for becoming decent adults, capable of working through problems, tolerating differences, resolving disagreements without violence.

It is too much to hope that we can live in perfect harmony all the time, but in *Siblings Without Rivalry*, Adele Faber and Elaine Mazlish describe their hopes for 'a world in which brothers and sisters grow up in homes where hurting isn't allowed; where children are taught to express their anger at each other sanely and safely; where each child is valued as an individual, not in relation to the others; where co-operation, rather than competition is the norm; where no one is trapped in a role; where children have daily experience and guidance in resolving their differences.'[12] It is a dream we surely all share.

'How are you?'   'Me?! Absolutely no idea, sorry.'

six

ALL ABOUT US

Motherhood brings with it a condition of conjunction, a sense of being accompanied, a feeling of being linked in to other people's existence. This is undoubtedly one of the greatest pleasures of parenthood, and one of its greatest privileges. What can compete with the trusting warmth of your own small child snuggled up on your lap, or the joyous reception you receive after just an hour's absence? Merely by existing, we matter. However ordinary and inconspicuous our lives, our children render us more important than all the world's presidents put together. It is the awareness of being needed by our children, necessary to them, loved and valued by them that gives purpose to our most mundane endeavours and constantly renews our own stamina for selfless loving. This is the part of parenthood that makes the hard work and broken nights bearable, the part that cannot easily be explained to people without children, the part that often seems mysteriously miraculous to ourselves.

In both delightful and daunting ways, our children are all about us. Physically, mentally, emotionally, spiritually. They are a non-negotiable condition of our existence. American anthropologist Sarah Blaffer Hrdy throws an interesting light on the special quality of the involvement between mothers and their children in her challenging and important book, *Mother Nature*, when she reflects on the deeper meanings of the culinary endearments mothers so often use with their children: 'muffin', 'cutie-pie', 'sausage', 'cup-cake', 'sweetie', 'sugar-plum'; 'honey-bun'. 'However delectable,' Blaffer Hrdy assures the reader, 'I am positive that I never had any inclination whatsoever to eat my children… My children's deliciousness rendered me more willing to be consumed *by them*, to give up bodily resources, and in my own contemporary example, most importantly, time… and so to subordinate my own aspirations to their desires so we could all (more or less) contentedly take our places at posterity's table.'[1]

When our children are young we are so absorbed by them, 'consumed by them' as Blaffer Hrdy puts it, so occupied by what mothering means on a day-to-day basis that there is little time to digest what it is about in more profound ways. In the welter of recurring daily needs, the deeper meanings of mothering are side-lined. There is seldom a moment to think about what our children, and the experience of mothering them, tell us about ourselves; it's the one story we never get round to: the one all about us. The thread of our own narrative becomes enmeshed with the astonishing forward-impetus of our children's lives. Sometimes we catch a glimpse of a woman in a shop window and we don't recognise her for a moment; we hear a voice talking to the children and just for a second we think it's our mother's voice we can hear.

In 1944 the *Ladies' Home Journal* described parenthood as 'that state of being better chaperoned than you were before marriage.' The bit about marriage may not have stood the test of time, but the rest of the definition is as true as it ever was. 'Even at bedtime I am not alone,' writes Melissa Benn in *Madonna and Child: Towards a New Politics of Motherhood*, 'that precious private time when once I was left with my own thoughts, swirling deliciously or dangerously around my head. Some part of my conscious and unconscious attention is now always with the little girl and then her baby sister, sleeping down the hallway.'[2] We may relish this sense of interconnection with our children, or we may find it alarming. We may feel both at different times. For mothering not only means frequent moments, *sublime* moments, of deep satisfaction, immense pleasure and heart-bursting pride, but also moments of the exact opposite. We love our children to the moon and back, just as Big Nut Brown Hare says, yet that is seldom the whole story. Adrienne Rich got closer to the truth in *Of Woman Born*:

> The bad and the good moments are inseparable for me... I remember early the sense of conflict, of a battleground none of us had chosen, of being an observer who, like it or not, was also an actor in an endless contest of wills... But I recall too each child's individual body, his slenderness, wiriness, softness, grace, the beauty of little boys who have not been taught that the male body must be rigid. I remember moments of peace when for some reason it was possible to go to the bathroom alone. I remember being uprooted from already meagre sleep to answer a childish nightmare, pull up a blanket, warm a consoling bottle, lead a half-asleep child to the toilet. I remember going back to bed starkly awake, brittle with anger, knowing that my broken sleep would make next day a hell, that there would be more nightmares, more need for consolation, because out of my weariness I would rage at those children for no reason they could understand.[3]

Precisely what makes the experience of mothering so difficult to convey is the continual co-existence of opposites: the wonderful and the awful; the calm and the chaotic; the tender and the violent; the love and the hate. In one of her short stories, Helen Simpson refers to 'the deep romance and boredom of it.' The phrase is shocking, but also apt. When Rozsika Parker writes that what mothers want our 'loving moments of at oneness' with their children, she means that we want respite from these contradictory impulses and emotions, and she is surely right, but what mothers also crave at times is not oneness, but *aloneness*. 'With two children' says Deborah, mother of Zoe and Caitlin 'I found there was no space for me. I felt grounded in a very positive way by my love for them, but I was also ground down by it at times. I felt surrounding, but also surrounded.' Even the saintly Mrs Ramsay, the literary embodiment of maternal selflessness in Virginia Woolf's *To the Lighthouse*, admits to feelings of relief when her family finally go to bed: 'For now she need not think about anybody. She could be herself, by herself. And that was what she often felt the need of. To think; well not even to think. To be silent; to be alone.'

If mothering means *not* being able to lose oneself, because one must always be there to anticipate and respond to the needs of others, it is also about *being* lost and not being able to find oneself. Often there's an uncomfortable sensation of invisibility that comes with mothering. Fiona, mother of Phoebe and Luke, recalls: 'Soon after I had my first child, a friend, who didn't have children, asked me if I felt invisible pushing a pram through the city centre like all the other women. But I didn't. I felt like me, pushing a pram through the city centre. But now I'm pushing two children through the city centre and yes, I feel invisible. I'm just another woman bogged down by children and pushchairs and shopping, rushing to get all my tasks done before one or both of the kids gets fed up.' In *What About Us? An Open Letter to the Mothers Feminism Forgot*, the author and journalist Maureen Freely wryly observes, 'It is no coincidence, that in more than half of the family photos in which I've appeared since having children, I've featured as a pair of arms holding a birthday cake.'[4] Asked why she never wrote poetry about being a mother, Adrienne Rich explained, 'For me, poetry was where I lived as no-one's mother, where I existed as myself.'[5]

But there is something seriously wrong here: our experiences of mothering are central to our sense of who we are – that must and ought to be so. It can't be right that being a mother should require us either to deny our sense of self, become invisible to others and ourselves, or deny our experiences of motherhood. It can't be right that what is at heart a powerfully enriching personal transformation so often becomes instead a prolonged exercise in self-denial.

Many women have told me that having their second child marked a fundamental shift from an adult-centred life to a child-centred one. 'With two children,' as one woman put it, 'you can't just carry on as before, in the way that you could with one child. You have to change pace and focus.' For many women this will be an entirely positive change, bringing with it a sense of fulfilment and purpose; for others it will an alarming experience of displacement; for most women it will be a mixture of the two.

In *The Mask of Motherhood*, Susan Maushart describes mothering as 'the most powerful of all biological capacities, and among the most disempowering of all social experiences.'[6] She argues that many women now mistakenly approach motherhood as a series of problems to be solved. 'We forget that… motherhood remains in essence precisely what it has always been: not a 'phase' or a 'challenge', not a 'hurdle' or an 'opportunity', but a way of life. It just so happens that it is a way of life utterly subversive to contemporary values stressing achievement, control and autonomy as the highest of adult aspirations.'[7] Becoming and being a mother of two children takes us deeper and further into that 'way of life' than ever. The increase in housework; the increase in calls on your attention; the increase in essential childcare chores; the increase in necessary child-related activities – all of these routine aspects of parenting make it vitally important to make time and space to meet your own needs and think your own thoughts.

Mother Strain and Why It Matters

'After I had my second child, I seemed to live under the kitchen table for about a year. I was always picking up cups and spoons and dropped biscuits,' says Charlotte, 32-year-old mother of Saskia and Flora. Celia, mother of Ben and Frances, echoes her sentiments: 'What I found difficult in that first year after Ben was born was how much more time I spent doing housework. I seemed to spend my whole time under the kitchen table or sweeping the floor, which I don't remember when it was just Frances.'

It's not boredom but kitchen-floordom that gets women down – the constant repetition of mundane tasks that need redoing so soon after being done, and bring no rewards other than the fleeting satisfaction of having done them, and which wear down one's sense of purpose, of effectiveness, of worth. According to marital therapist Susan Harrison: 'This is the most frustrating period in a woman's life. You are giving, giving, giving all day long, but no one seems to be giving anything to you in return. Even your partner isn't always able to give you what you need. It is very important not to set yourself unrealistically high expectations.' Yet because we don't know very much about how anyone else is doing this thing we call 'mothering', it can be hard to know what our expectations should be exactly. 'Fifty years ago,' Brian Waller from Home Start points out, 'most women would have encountered babies all the time as they were growing up. For most people nowadays, the first baby they meet at close quarters is their own.'

It's easy to think you are the only one not coping; the only one who screams at her children; the only one whose kids throw tantrums at the supermarket check-out; the only one to feel her heart sinking as her partner leaves for work in the morning and there are still two hours to go until Tellytubbies; the only one to feel her heart soaring guiltily when it is she who walks out of the front door, with no one for company but her handbag.

With our first child we can just about live up to the standards set in the baby books; if we fall short, at least there's time to read up on the problem. With our second child, particularly in the first year or two, there's barely time to brush our teeth never mind monitor, assess or modify our mothering technique. 'The worst thing was the broken nights,' says Jane, mother of Helena and Jessica, now aged seven and five. 'Both girls woke at night several times a week until they were four, and they still wake from time to time even now. We haven't had more than ten unbroken nights since they were born, and there were times when they were very small when it was so bad I thought I would go mad from tiredness. I'd be up three or four times in the night with Jessica, and then Helena would wake at six and want breakfast. What's weird is that, although I know other people's children wake in the night, no one talks about it. There's this feeling that you're somehow failing as a parent if your children don't sleep through, so people stop talking about it. They talk about nothing else in the first three months and then – silence!'

Sleep – lack of it – is one feature of parenthood that you think can't possibly get worse after the first child, and then discover that actually it can. Eight hours is the recommended nightly dose, and falling short by even one hour a night has a detectable impact on IQ; two hours' shortfall a night and you're 15 IQ points down. My younger siblings often complain that their older brothers and sisters have become 'dead boring' since having children, but it's hardly surprising, is it? With around 20 years of broken nights between us, we're losing IQ points like sieves lose water. 'In families with two or more children, the period in which a mother can expect to have her rest routinely interrupted can last for ten or more years,' writes Maushart. 'This is outrageous, but it is also perfectly 'normal.'[8] She contrasts the 'night-time reality of broken sleep' with the public myth that 'once a baby learns to 'sleep through' by three or four or six months, the problem has been solved.'

Sleep has become the major preoccupation of parents in recent years, as the sales of books such as Richard Ferber's *Solve Your Child's Sleep Problems* show. There are now clinics all over Britain that specialise in 'training' children to sleep through the night. The London-based agency, Night Nannies, provides a 9.00pm to 7.00am service for parents who can't (or don't want to) do the night shift. Part of the service offered by Night Nannies is teaching babies and children to sleep at night, or at least not to wake their parents. According to an experienced health visitor I spoke to, concern about how children sleep is a fairly recent phenomenon that is fast becoming an obsession. 'Twenty years ago the problems were all to do with feeding. Parents were tremendously anxious about what their children should eat, and when, and how often. Now parents have stopped worrying so much about food and instead they are obsessed by sleep. It's what we get asked about more than anything else. Afternoon naps, bedtime tantrums, night-time wakings, early mornings. It's the big concern of modern parents.'

What may very well lie behind this change in parental preoccupations in the last 20 years is the dramatic change in women's employment patterns. Not only are eight out of ten mothers now in paid employment, but the biggest change has been among women with the youngest children. Thirty years ago, only 27 per cent of mothers with children under the age of five were in paid employment; now more than half are combining young children with paid work outside the home. More mothers are now working, and they're working when their children are younger: 20 years ago 24 per cent of mothers returned to work within a year of childbirth compared to 67 per cent by 1996; in addition, a third of these mothers were returning to full-time jobs, compared to just 7 per cent in 1979. At the same time, the proportion of couples with dependent children where *both* parents are working has also risen steadily. Taken together, these trends are driving down our tolerance for broken nights.

Anastasia Cooke, founder of Night Nannies, set up the agency after she had her second child and was struggling to hold down a demanding job in television with a wakeful new baby. She quickly discovered she was not alone. With two-thirds of couples with dependent children now both going out to work, sleep has become the Achilles heel of the modern family. If you've both got to be at the office in the morning, broken nights matter. You may be able to drag yourself to the toy library and back on three hours' sleep, but it's much harder to get through an important meeting, or meet a tight deadline. Children *must* sleep through the night from 12 weeks, because otherwise their parents simply won't be able to cope at work the next day. Never mind that many children won't settle into a regular pattern of sleeping at night until they're two or three at least.

A significant proportion of women who go back to work after their first child then leave their jobs or cut back their hours after they have their second. This pattern has caused much head-scratching among social scientists, who see all too clearly the disastrous impact of leaving work or going part-time on a woman's earnings, promotion prospects and retirement pay. But the mystery factor pushing women out of the workplace may be nothing more mysterious than the horrendous toll of broken nights, and the strain of carrying on regardless. Pulling back on work may not make children sleep any better, but it does make broken nights more bearable.

When Robert Stewart looked at the impact of second children on 40 American couples, he found that both mothers and fathers experienced having a second child as a positive, but very stressful event in their lives. A surprisingly large number of the mothers had levels of stress 'high enough to warrant possible [medical] intervention'.[9] Another survey, by the Joseph Rowntree Foundation, discovered that a woman's life satisfaction drops to an all-time low in the year after the birth of her second child. While many women find motherhood pleasurable and rewarding, it is clear that many others find it extremely hard going. We're not talking here about a one-off transition to motherhood, but about the accumulating experience of being a mother. Studies from America, Germany, Britain and Israel have found that the mental and physical health of mothers deteriorates as their family size increases. Mothers of under-fives have more mental health problems, and are more likely to suffer from anxiety, stress and depression than women of the same age who either do not have children, or whose children are older. Mothers of under-fives also have worse mental health than fathers of under-fives.

The trend towards having our children later may be exacerbating the difficulties that many women experience when their children are young. Women in their thirties have had longer to grow accustomed to being in control of their lives, which may make the sudden requirement to give up the habits of their entire adulthood harder than they anticipated. Pointing to evidence that older women are more at risk of mental health problems, particularly in the initial period of adjustment to motherhood, Maushart has argued that 'A woman accustomed to taking autonomy for granted may find the experience of newborn motherhood strangely claustrophobic as she struggles to fit two people into a space formerly reserved for one.'[10]

The adjustment to motherhood is not an isolated event, however, something that happens only after the birth of the first child; rather, it is an adjustment made by degrees with each child, and as many women discover, the space that was formerly reserved for one adult becomes still more of a squash when shared with not one child, but two. Looked at this way, we shouldn't be in the least surprised that parents, and particularly mothers, report high levels of stress in the year after the birth of their second child. Really, there's nothing surprising about it at all, other than how overlooked it is.

The Hidden Depths

Sometimes the normal levels of tiredness and exasperation can tip over into something more serious. Feelings of despair, lethargy, irritability, anxiety and depression are all indications that a woman may be suffering from post-natal depression. Because we tend to think of mothering as something that should come naturally, the realisation that we are not coping may bring feelings of guilt, shame and self-loathing. The discovery that being a happy fulfilled mother does not necessarily come at all naturally is a terrible blow to our self-esteem and confidence. Many women, not surprisingly, go to great lengths to conceal their despair from the outside world, and yet, as statistics show, taking unnaturally to motherhood is pretty normal.

Post-natal depression can start any time during the first year after childbirth and last anything from a few weeks to many years. It differs from typical depression, both in its symptoms (although there is overlap) and in its cause. Post-natal depression can affect any woman, regardless of age, weight, height, intelligence or class. It can take various forms and may be mildly debilitating or severe enough to necessitate hospitalisation. Ten days after giving birth to her second child, Fiona Shaw descended into a severe post-natal depression. She was happily married, had had no problems of this kind after her first child, and her second pregnancy had gone entirely smoothly. There was very little in her immediate circumstances to suggest that she might be vulnerable to post-natal depression, and yet two weeks after giving birth she was an in-patient on a mother-and-baby ward at a psychiatric hospital, where she was to remain, under constant supervision, for the next three months. Shaw later published an account of this terrifying experience in her book *Out of Me*. She describes the bewilderment she felt at her rapid descent into deep depression.

> The woman who began that week, returning home triumphant
> with her second child, was not the person there at the end of it,
> or so it seemed. Where did I go to, or come from? Was the despair
> I felt when Jesse was ten days old something I had lived with

unwittingly? Or something invented out of the blue in that short hour of my baby's life?[11]

When full-blown post-natal depression or post-natal psychosis takes hold, there is no ignoring it. Ordinary life, ordinary pretending, is not possible. Hallucinations, delusions, manic behaviour, paranoid fantasies are all features of puerperal psychosis. Under the influence of these delusions, a woman may try to harm or even kill herself or her baby, and immediate medical intervention is needed for the safety of both. It is a terrifying experience for a woman and her family to go through and in virtually all cases of post-natal psychosis, a woman will need treatment in hospital. Fortunately, severe post-natal depression affects only about one in every 200 to 500 births. Far more common and far less recognised is a level of misery that women try to conceal both from themselves and from everyone else, a level of suffering that is very real, but can be hidden behind closed doors and drawn curtains, a level of distress that thousands of women heroically and mistakenly try to cope with alone and in secret.

Post-natal depression is thought to affect around 20 per cent of mothers. Although research findings suggest that women are most at risk after the birth of their first child, this may simply reflect the fact that women are much less likely to report it with their second child unless the symptoms are very severe. Kate Figes points out in *Life After Birth,* that 'the true incidence is probably far higher, for post-natal depression is often missed or misdiagnosed since it can be provoked or compounded by unavoidable aspects of motherhood such as exhaustion, poor health and changes in marital relations. Women are often reluctant or simply too tired to consult doctors. Sometimes they do not know that they are depressed until they emerge from the fog and look back on those grey days.'[12]

Up to 80 per cent of women will experience the 'baby blues', a short-lived phase that starts soon after giving birth and lasts only a few days, while at the other end of the spectrum, one in 500 will suffer from its full-blown version, puerperal psychosis, which may last for months, can be fatal and always requires a period of hospitalisation. The majority of women – certainly many more than the official figure of 20 per cent – will experience something in between the two. As Figes says, 'Post-natal depression hovers in the huge chasm between these two extremes of mild "baby blues" and psychosis. It can be liveable with or debilitating, and when women are strongly affected the feelings of self-blame are often the worst aspect.'[13]

Fiona, mother of Phoebe and Luke, was diagnosed with post-natal depression with both her children. 'I had been depressed after I had Phoebe, but I didn't really expect it to happen again. When I did become depressed after Luke was born, I didn't want to admit it to myself, but the health visitors picked up on it very quickly and I was referred to a specialist and prescribed antidepressants, which I think helped. I started to feel better after about nine months, but those first nine months were very, very hard. I felt so ashamed for not coping, like all the other mothers seemed to be doing. To begin with I used to go along to the baby clinics at the doctor's surgery, but the other women seemed to be finding it so easy. I remember one woman actually saying, 'It's much easier second time round, isn't it?' I just said, 'Oh, yes,' but it made me feel such a failure. I stopped going after that. In fact, I didn't really see much of anyone that year. At home, I couldn't cope with the housework at all. The books all tell you to rest when the baby sleeps and not to rush round doing the housework, but who is going to do it if you don't? It's not like some angel comes in the night while you're sleeping. In fact I was too depressed to do the housework, but I kept trying to reassure myself that it was OK because the books said I shouldn't. But that meant the house was a complete pigsty, which only added to my feeling of being completely out of control. My partner was wonderful, really supportive, but that was almost like another pressure: I was scared that he would run out of patience any minute. It just felt like there was a huge time bomb ticking away, due to explode any minute – and all because I was such a failure.'

When women do not live up to their own and other people's expectations, they tend to blame themselves, to see it as *their* failure. Instead of asking for extra help from friends of family, or seeking professional support from GPs or health visitors, they are more inclined to present a brave face to the world, or else retreat from social situations altogether. Charlotte realised she was depressed about four months after the birth of her second child, Saskia. 'I'd been fine with my first child, and it took me by surprise to be feeling so low after my second, especially since it had been a much easier, natural birth, whereas my son had been born by emergency Caesarean section. But coping with two children was much harder than I'd anticipated, and then my father died when Saskia was just a few weeks old, and everything just got too much for me. By the time she was four months, I was completely drained, crying all the time, losing my patience with Flora, overwhelmed by the housework. My husband was very worried, he kept saying, 'Where's the woman I married?', but I couldn't tell him. I didn't know myself. Whenever people came round, or if we went to their house, I put on a front of being absolutely fine, so no one outside the family had any idea what I was going through. Eventually I went to see my doctor, who prescribed a course of Prozac, which I found really helped. That first year was really the hardest. Now life seems to have settled down into a new rhythm and it feels a lot easier.'

Post-natal depression in its mild or severe forms usually begins in the first few weeks after giving birth. It is different from the 'baby blues', which very commonly occurs three to five days after a woman has given birth. Whereas the baby blues is a short-lived episode of feeling very emotional, weepy and easily upset that lasts no more than a few days, post-natal depression is longer-lasting and characterised by deepening and unshakeable feelings of despair, disorientation and distress. It may start within hours of the birth, or set in gradually in the course of several weeks.

Every year an estimated 23,000 women will be mildly depressed after the birth of a child. If your second child is more than six weeks old and you are experiencing any of the above symptoms more of the time than not, speak to your GP or health visitor. They may suggest counselling, psychotherapy, anti-depressants, or hormone therapy. There is some evidence that for women who are mildly to moderately depressed a mix of medication, counselling and self-help works best.

One common symptom of post-natal depression is exhaustion. However, exhaustion can also have a straightforward physical cause, such as a malfunctioning thyroid (sometimes caused by the hormonal changes after giving birth, easy to detect and easy to treat), anaemia (common after childbirth, particularly if there was haemorrhaging during delivery), or potassium deficiency (diagnosed by a simple blood test and remedied by eating potassium-rich foods, such as bananas, tomatoes and orange juice, or taking potassium tablets). Ask your doctor to investigate these possibilities.

Post-natal Depression

The causes of post-natal depression are not clear but the following can help reduce the risk of developing it:

- Practical and emotional support.
- Time with other adults, with or without children.
- Enough sleep.
- Regular exercise.
- Time off from children and housework on a regular basis.
- Realistic expectations of yourself, your children and your partner.

Common symptoms are:

- Feeling exhausted.
- Feeling inadequate.
- Not being able to cope.
- Bursts of irrational irritability and anger.
- Loss of pleasure in life generally, or activities you used to enjoy.
- Emotional flatness.
- Crying and tearfulness.
- Feeling very anxious (including panic attacks, palpitations, sweating).
- Indifference or coldness towards baby.
- Loss of appetite.
- Loss of concentration.
- Thoughts about death or dying.

Post-natal psychosis is relatively rare, affecting one in 500 births, but it is a serious condition and can be fatal, for either the mother or the baby. If you have any of the symptoms below, you should seek help from your GP immediately:

- Extreme irritability.
- Feeling speeded up.
- Not needing sleep or rest.
- Distractibility.
- Speaking very quickly, tripping over words.
- Excitability.
- Delusions or visions.

(Adapted from *Surviving the Baby Blues* by Jane Feinmann.)

What causes the depression that hits so many women after the birth of a child is still not clear, but it's very likely a combination of factors. Many people believe that depression in mothers is caused by the experience of mothering itself, by the conditions in which we currently mother, and the emotional repression that is expected of us. Rozsika Parker argues in *Torn in Two* that mothers become depressed because of the unrealistic and unsupportive cultural climate in which they do their mothering. 'The idealisation of oneness, the representation of mothers as good or bad rather than inevitably ambivalent, the frequent absence of previous experience of childcare, the often sole responsiblity, the social isolation, and the eruption of emotions considered unacceptable in mothers, all combine to produce the feelings of helplesslensss so closely associated with the inability to transform aggression into creative care and attention.'[14]

Whether the stresses of mothering are caused by sociological factors, such as lack of support and inflexible working hours, or psychological factors, such as low self-esteem and repressed anger, or physical factors, such as sleep deprivation, or most probably a combination of all these, one thing is sure: women do not suffer in isolation, however much it feels that way to them, because when a mother is depressed, stressed or merely (*merely*!) exhausted, the rest of her family suffers too. For that reason alone, mother-strain deserves to be taken seriously.

Parents as Partners: Why Your Relationship Counts

A mother's mental state has an impact on her children's well-being, whether she works or stays at home. Maternal depression has been linked to poor concentration, social withdrawal, aggression and low academic achievement in children. When Ellen Galinksy and her colleagues at the Families and Work Institute in New York looked at what children want from their parents, they heard a striking consensus of opinion. Children didn't mind whether their parents worked or not; what they disliked was their parents being stressed, distracted, exhausted and bad-tempered as a result of working.[15] The message from these children was clear: it's not what you do, it's the way that you do it.

Men ,similarly, are not immune to their partner's mental state. Dr Malcolm George has pointed out that 'while distress in relationships can result in depression, depression can lead to increased levels of distress in

Looking After Number One

The five golden rules are:

- Get enough exercise: Taking time to walk, cycle, swim, run, do an exercise class, or workout at the gym will help to relieve physical tension as well as boost your energy levels. Reseach shows that the most beneficial activities are those that combine exercise, company and stimulation (for example, dancing and ski-ing). When people do activities with these three components, they not only feel better, they also cope better with the stresses and strains of daily life.
- Get enough sleep. Many of us get by on six hours a night, but eight is what most of actually need. Less than this, and our IQ starts to fall, along with our concentration, temper control, coordination and general sense of well-being.
- Have some fun: by yourself, with your partner, with your friends, and above all, with your children. Dance, sing, play the piano, dress up. If you can't stand being you, try pretending to be someone else for a while, like the ogre from *Jack and the Beanstalk*, or the wolf from *Little Red Riding Hood*, or even the fairy godmother in *Cinderella*. Good old-fashioned laughter has been shown to reduce stress and boost the immune system.
- Take time to relax. Many GP practices have health visitors who can teach relaxation techniques. Yoga, meditation, massage and aromatherapy can all help with relaxation.
- Indulge yourself. Regular, if only occasional, bouts of pampering are a priority. It doesn't matter what you do, so long as you really enjoy it: an hour in a cafe with a cup of coffee and a Sunday paper; an evening out with friends or partner; a good film; a facial. One woman I spoke to had her eyelashes dyed when her second child was fourteen months old. She said the boost it gave her every time she looked in the mirror was well worth the expense.

relationships. The interactions of a couple where one partner is depressed show greater conflict, tension and negative expressiveness.'[16] Studies in the UK of men whose partners are suffering from post-natal depression have found that 40 per cent of those men also showed symptoms of depression, while a startling *50 per cent* of husbands whose wives were hospitalised with depression became clinically depressed themselves.[17]

Stress too can have a knock-on effect from one partner to another, and it has been shown that mothers who go out to work are less at risk of depression than full-time mothers, but more prone to stress and exhaustion, both of which can take a toll on marriages.

For parents, the significance of all this is that children are directly affected by the happiness or otherwise of the adults' relationship. The latest findings from the Cowans' research in California, based on 200 families in 28 cities, is that the emotional and mental health of the parents, and the state of their relationship, is a key factor in determining how happy their children are. Happy adults lead to happy children. Yet the Cowans found that within the first six years of their first child's birth, one in four parents indicated serious levels of depression, and one in two indicated serious marital strain. Their research showed that even parents who had successfully navigated the transition from being a couple to being a family after the birth of their first child, saw marital difficulties soar between the third and fifth year of that child's life, by which time, of course, many of them had gone on to have a second child. As Philip Cowan concludes, 'Parenting takes place in the context of families, [but] couples need help and support in managing the challenges of family life, for themselves and for their children.'[18]

Second-time parents are often surprised to discover how much strain a second child puts on their adult relationship. Even though most of us discovered after the birth of our first child that children and coupledom are about as compatible as cats and dogs, most of us seem equally unprepared for the impact of our second child. Perhaps by the time we have our second child we imagine that the damage has been done, or that we've done all the adjusting necessary, or that knowing what we're letting ourselves in for is the same as being able to handle it. Whatever our private thoughts on the matter, the arrival of a second child will often mark a critical stage in a couple's relationship. 'There's simply no question,' declares 34-year-old Laura, a historian and mother-of-two. 'The real casualty of children is marriage. David and I have very little time for ourselves. We don't even argue any more because we don't spend enough time in each other's company to have anything to argue about. He's busy, I'm busy. We're both flat out. We don't even try to sleep in the same bed at the moment. I sleep with the baby, David sleeps in the spare bed. After my first child that would have really bothered me. Now I know it's the best solution to the broken nights. I know it's only for a short time. We went on to conceive our second child; we'll be in the same bed again. I've learnt not to expect too much. Not to make emotional demands. I just keep reminding myself that he's a good husband and really is doing his best.'

'You just have to keep working at it,' says Janice. 'It's very easy to let the adult relationship slip out of the picture. Weeks go past and you haven't had a proper conversation, and then you wake up several years later thinking, who is this person?' When Janice and her husband realised this was happening to them, they decided to commit one night a week to going out together. 'We won't always spend it alone, sometimes we'll meet up with friends, but knowing that there's one night each week for us is great. It helps us stay in touch with each other. It's easy to forget you're a wife, or husband, as well as a parent.'

Children don't so much create pressure on marriage as play upon pre-existing fault lines. This is also the view of Christopher Clulow, Director of the Tavistock Marital Studies Institute. 'One of the consistent research findings is that the relationship between couple satisfaction and children is U- or W-shaped. The lowest trough is in the pre-school years. If a second child follows closely on the first, that will add to the dip. It's not that children create problems, but that becoming a parent reactivates experiences of being a child, so you have to ask what is the meaning of a second child for the adults who make up that particular couple?' If there is strain within the couple's relationship before they have children, there are likely to be more problems afterwards too, and for these couples the second child is almost bound to exacerbate, not ameliorate the situation.

But this does not explain why even couples who have had a good relationship prior to having children can find themselves in trouble. 'Having children may nor may not enrich a marriage,' writes Susan Maushart. 'But there is no doubt at all that it will put our notions of partnership to a test which will spell failure for many, and disillusion for most... Determining whether the rewards of parenting ultimately outweigh the costs to the relationship is a calculation men and women tend to make separately – and in secret.'[19]

For many women, the calculation is not about the rewards of parenting, but about the rewards of *partnering*. With a second child, we not only become more deeply embedded in the task of mothering than before, but there is also a growing awareness of being embedded in the parental relationship. Depending on the individual woman and her circumstances, this may be a welcome development, or a terrifying one. 'I suddenly realised that there was no way out', says Fiona, 'that I was in this relationship, with this man, for years and years to come. Whatever happened between us, we were stuck together. I couldn't just walk out because I couldn't deprive the children of their father, or him of them. I don't know why this only dawned on me after my second child was born, but I suddenly saw the future for the first time, and it was really frightening!'

Deborah, mother of Zoe and Caitlin, thinks this happens for a great many parents after they have their second child. 'Every couple I know is in crisis', she says. 'Obviously they're not all about to split up, but they're all having to look pretty seriously at their relationship. It's something to do with the second child, the extra strain it puts on the woman, the extra strain on the couple. I think it's when you have your second child that you really hit reality. You have to confront the choices that you've made.'

Parents tend to downplay the significance of their relationship for their children's happiness. In particular, we seem keen to play ostrich when it comes to the effects on children of parental conflict. A survey of just over 2,000 adults, conducted by MORI in 1999 for the National Family and Parenting Institute in London, found that even though three-quarters of us think that our parents have influenced the way we ourselves parent, only a third of us thinks it matters if parents are getting on together.[20] Interestingly, nearly half of these parents reported having had problems in their relationships with their own partner or spouse. Clearly it suits a lot of us to imagine that children don't notice or don't care what we get up to between ourselves, so as long as we mind our 'p's and 'q's in our dealings with them. We are, of course, seriously deluding ourselves. Warring parents, whether they're still married or long since separated, are bad for children's well-being.

It is not conflict itself that is bad for children, but the nature, intensity and subject of conflict. Evidence reviewed by the organisation One Plus One, together with psychologist Dr Gordon Harold,[21] has revealed that *how* parents resolve conflict can make a real difference to its impact on children. As Penny Mansfield of One Plus One explains, many parents start arguments in front of the children, but finish them in private. 'Children are often excluded from the resolution of the argument, but if they only ever see their parents arguing and never see them making up, they will become anxious and insecure. Because children find parental conflict stressful, it's important that they see their parents resolving arguments. This is also how they learn to handle conflict themselves.'

Around 160,000 children aged under 16 experienced divorce in their family in 1995; almost one-third were children under five. Divorce rates have stayed steady in recent years, but are nevertheless among the highest in Europe. It has been estimated that nearly 20 per cent of children born to married couples will experience parental divorce by the time they're ten, and overall around one in five children have to endure their parents' separation or divorce. Research findings on the effects of divorce and separation on children are contradictory. When compared with children of parents who are still together, children of parents who've separated are more likely to have behavioural problems such as bed-wetting, aggression and delinquency; they do less well at school and get fewer qualifications; they have more accidents and more health problems; they are more likely to become sexually active at an early age, to get pregnant, to leave school at an early age, to suffer from depression, drug and alcohol abuse in adolescence, and to earn less in adulthood. However, the *majority* of children of divorced parents do not experience these negative effects.

What we don't know is whether these problems are caused by divorce and separation, or by circumstances that predate the separation or arise afterwards. Divorce can leave separated parents worse off financially, as well as depressed and anxious. Since divorced parents often remarry, children of divorced parents frequently find themselves with a step-parent and perhaps some step-siblings or half-siblings to cope with as well. Parents in step-families meanwhile are more prone to depression, and both step-parents and biological parents have more relationship problems and more conflicts over child-rearing than non-step-families.[22]

A further problem for children of divorced or separated parents is that a great many of them will lose contact, either gradually or abruptly, with one parent, usually their father, and this loss can itself be a source of great distress and the cause of a range of behavioural and educational difficulties in children. For children, 'parental separation is a time of crisis, the effects of which stayed with them for many years',[23] but rather than trying to pin the blame on divorce *per se*, Bryan Rogers and Jan Pryor, authors of a report on the outcomes of parental separation for children, suggest that it makes more sense to see divorce as 'a process, rather than a single event'.

It is vital not to see divorce as the sole cause of difficulties for children. Divorce is not good for kids, but conflict is not good for kids either. When parents manage to divorce without getting dragged into painful acrimonious battles, children adjust better than they do when parents carry on fighting during and after their separation. On the other hand, numerous studies have suggested that marital conflict *before* the divorce may be as much to blame for children's problems afterwards as the divorce itself.

While the misery of being in a relationship that is going badly cannot be overestimated, it is vital to remember, as psychiatrist Anthony Clare points out, that 'People's satisfaction with their marriages and their families makes by far the greatest contribution to their happiness: much greater than that made by job or money.'[24] Instead of plotting escape routes (one friend of mine believes all wives are secret 'mind murderers', even if we're entertaining nothing more than a gentle fantasy about sudden heart attacks and having the mortgage paid off), we need to be planning how to protect ourselves and our relationships from the inevitable stresses and strains of parenting. We need to be asking ourselves what we can do to ease the strain, minimise the conflict, reduce the toll on ourselves, our partners and our children.

The Importance of Fathers

Perhaps the first thing we can do is recognise the real value of fathering. As a culture, we are down on men: they are characterised as clownish dead-beats at one end of the spectrum, dangerous predators at the other. In his book *On Men: Masculinity in Crisis*, Anthony Clare observes that 'So much is written about the importance of the mother, and understandably so. But our fears and fantasies, expectations and idealisations of fathers are rich, complex and formative too. We can be as shaped by the father we never had as by the father who is ever present.'[25] Clare bemoans the erosion of paternal status in family life over the last 200 years or so, which he traces in part to the process of industrialisation, which had the effect of pushing fathers out into workplaces that were distinct from and distant from the home and children. Social and economic changes during the last century that have transformed women's lives have further compounded the problem for men. Fathers, Clare laments, are in danger of becoming utterly redundant; they spend less and less time with their children as they put in ever longer hours at work; they still don't pull their weight in the house; their wives think they're better off without them, and in many cases they're right, and technological advances in fertility treatment mean they're no longer even needed at conception.

But a growing body of research also suggests that fathers do matter. As Clare and others are at pains to point out, men have a crucial role to play in family life. During early childhood, the presence of a loving, involved, supportive father helps a boy to form a positive masculine self-image that will last him a lifetime. Boys learn from their father's example during their childhood not only how to be male, but also how to be, or not to be, a father. They learn how to handle their strength and anger in acceptable ways that don't involve physically hurting other people. They learn, if they're lucky, how to be friends with women in general, and how to be emotionally and sexually intimate with some women in particular. Having an involved father may also make a difference to a boy's educational development and academic achievement. Boys who enjoy a close emotional bond with their fathers are also less at risk of delinquency in adolescence.[26] For girls, too, fathers can be a beneficial influence, enhancing their sense of physical confidence, raising their self-esteem, boosting social and professional aspirations, and nurturing their ability in adolescence to separate from their mothers.[27] 'Fatherhood remains a central civilising force in every society,' writes Anthony Clare. 'The responsibilities, opportunities, duties, emotional demands and rewards involved in being a father can and, in many cases, do help young males' – and I would add, young females – 'develop into mature, constructive and caring social beings.'[28] To the architects of American society, where 40 per cent of boys do not live with their fathers, such assertions, backed up by compelling research, are a huge warning bell. In Britain, too, an increasing number of children grow up without their fathers. The proportion of children brought up in lone-parent families shot up from 6 per cent in 1972 to 18 per cent in 1996; around 21 per cent of families in

Britain are now being headed by a lone parent, nearly always a mother. These children may be better off without their fathers if they are feckless or violent, but children still need strong male role-models if they are to bypass the pitfalls of adolescence and develop into assured, capable adults.

Fathers themselves tend to see their importance in traditional terms, as providers and disciplinarians, but this is not what children nor mothers necessarily want from them and certainly not *all* they want from them.[29] Children want their fathers to spend time with them, to talk to them, to be interested in them, as well as to give them their pocket money, run a taxi service and draw the line from time to time. Women, on the other hand, want something more nebulous: we want our partners to be 'involved', by which we mean psychologically engaged and available just as much as actually bodily present and able.

Janice, mother of Gareth and Eva, has been a part-time teacher since her children were quite young. Of her husband, she says musingly, 'I don't think I actually want Jonathan there, cooking supper five times a week, shovelling laundry into the washing machine – though that would be nice! – what I want is the feeling that he's on the case, that he is thinking about us while he's out at work, and that if I really needed him for anything he wouldn't hesitate, because we're his number one priority. I want to feel that he cares about the girls and wants to know them as people in their own right.'

Gloria Steinem once famously remarked that what every woman wants is a wife. I used to agree with her, but I'm not so sure any more. Many women I spoke to did not want to be duplicated, they did not want their men to become pseudo-women about the house, so that they could become pseudo-men at work; they especially didn't want men trespassing on their emotional territory as mothers. We may have welcomed our husbands into the kitchen (something our mothers' generation found – still find – hard) but we categorically do not want them colonising the corner of our children's hearts that is forever mummy's. In *Ending the Mother War*, Jayne Buxton expresses similar concerns about the ideal of absolute equality between men and women, what she calls the 'Myth of the New Father': 'The Myth of the New Father has within it some important grains of truth. One of these is that truly shared parenting will be the best thing that can possibly happen to women, children and fathers.

Another is that real commitment to childcare by fathers is a source of immense support to women pursuing demanding careers. But we... will be sadly disappointed if we expect that the New Father can ever be synonymous with "mother" replacing us within the home and in our children's eyes, without anyone noticing the difference. We are not wrong to want men to become New Fathers, not mistaken in thinking that New Fathers are good for children, mothers, even themselves. But the host of assumptions surrounding the belief in the New Father – assumptions about what he can and can't do, how he will change women's and families' lives, and how he will actually become a New Father in the first place – need to be re-examined.'[30]

Women value paternal involvement very highly, in fact *twice* as highly as fathers themselves do. Furthermore, the more involved with their children a woman feels her partner is, the happier she is with her marriage and with her life in general.[31] The good news for women and men, not to mention children, is that a 1999 survey found that fathers are now doing far more with their children. They're helping with hobbies, housework, schoolwork; they're taking their children into work, to the park, to play football; they're going to museums together, walking the dog, washing up, going to restaurants.[32] The amount of time that British fathers spend with their children has gone up by 400 per cent since the 1960s according to some estimates.

A growing number of men *want* to be involved and effective fathers to their children, partners to their wives and partners, and after their second child is born, many fathers *do* become more involved than they were after their first. Robert Stewart found clear evidence that second-time fathers were more interested and involved with their children than they had been first time round. With that increased involvement, however, came increased stress. Stewart found that, 'although mothers experienced both higher levels of stress and a wider range of stressors than their spouses did, the fathers also experienced the birth of their second child as a stressful event.'[33] Stewart's explanation for this was that as fathers became more involved with the daily care of children, they also became more aware, and more prey to, the 'sources of stress already known to the mothers.'[34] To put it another way, as men are drawn into the lives of small children, they discover what their partners had been complaining about.

Not that this is much of a consolation to women. 'I sometimes wonder if it wouldn't be better to do things the way my parents did,' says Caroline, mother of Tom and Bridget. 'I mean, we're all trying to do everything now, aren't we? But it's not easy, trying to job-share life.'

Caroline may well be right, but she needn't worry too much. I've encountered plenty of men who have happily stood chatting in my kitchen while I scrambled round trying to feed two hungry, fractious children and wondered why they didn't push off home to help with their own children – until it dawned on me: these guys didn't want to get home until their own kids were safely tucked up in bed. Fathers of children under five currently work the longest hours outside the home of any group of male employees. Is this bread-winner anxiety, caused by the drop in family income as the woman's earnings fall or stop altogether, or a home-avoidance strategy?

Removed from the day-to-day realities of parenting small children, fathers can if they want remain blithely unaware of all the extra work that comes with a second child. Celia recalls, 'The day after Ben was born, I took him and Frances to the swings, while Peter sat reading the paper. That night I had them both in bed with me while he went to sleep in the spare room, and the next morning I was up with them both at 6.00am. My mum rang at about eight and said, "I hope he's looking after you, I hope you're getting some rest", whereas I was actually just about to take him up a cup of tea. I wanted to burst into tears. He was absolutely useless with our first child, and only a little better with our second.'

With all the talk about single mothers, remarkably few politicians, economists, sociologists or journalists seem to realise that *most* mothers are single mothers from Monday to Friday. Natalie's husband works in the City; he leaves for the office before 7.00am and is never back before 8.00pm. He doesn't see his children at all during the week, and she won't get any domestic or child-related help from him until the weekend. Natalie enjoys substantially more material perks than we tend to think of as a single mother, but in terms of responsibility for her children, there's not much between them.

Even women who are committed to the idea of equality usually find that once their second child is born, roles become more polarised: mothers do more housework, more childcare, less paid work; fathers do less housework, less childcare and earn more of the household's income.

Couples who are happy to split roles along traditional lines, like Natalie and her husband, are generally more content with their relationship once children arrive than couples who continue to strive for an egalitarian life-style. According to Christopher Clulow, this is because 'egalitarian couples are often thrown back on traditional, segregated roles once children arrive, even if they don't want to be. This knocks their ideals of egalitarian status within the relationship and also knocks their sense of how things ought to be. It's a double whammy. Some couples will cope better with these challenges to their identity than others.'

Ruth and her husband divide roles along traditional lines, even though Ruth remains committed to her work as an architect. She sees this as a short-term arrangment while the children are very young. 'James earns the money, I get to be at home with the children – much nicer!' she tells me. 'When we had our first child, he made it clear he wouldn't be doing much with the baby – and he was as good as his word! He did nothing at all to help with Hannah when she was little, and that was a very hard year for me. But by the time Rachel was born, he had a real relationship with Hannah, and she often wanted him, not me, so he got drawn into helping with the children in a way that really made a difference to me. I did everything first time round; but second time round he was much more involved; we were much more of a team.' Ruth was basically happy with the role division between herself and James, but needed more support after her first child was born. With her second child, she got more support, so the strain she'd experienced with her first child was not repeated or increased.

This is certainly not the case for all couples though. Charlotte and her husband, Nigel, had an egalitarian marriage before they had children, and both assumed that would continue unchanged, although in retrospect, Charlotte wonders if she assumed this more than Nigel did. 'I didn't earn as much as Nigel, but that was the only real inequality between us before we had Flora. I enjoyed my maternity leave after she was born, but always planned to go back to work, which I did when she was six months old. A large chunk of my earnings went on childcare costs, but it meant that Nigel and I were still equal more or less. When Anna was born, though, it all went haywire. I couldn't afford to keep working at the same level because my childcare costs had doubled, so I ended up doing far more childcare and domestic stuff, and feeling very frustrated and sidelined as a result. It caused an enormous amount of tension. Our marriage was very rocky for a long time.'

Couples with the greatest degree of marital satisfaction are the ones in the most traditional marriages with the most clearly divided roles. The women in these marriages, however, show greatest signs of strain at an individual level, with higher levels of depression and lower self-esteem. In contrast, the women who combine paid work and mothering are more stressed and markedly less satisfied with their marriages, but have better mental health than their stay-at-home counterparts. Perhaps all that this reflects is that charting new waters is stressful, but still a predominantly positive challenge. Then again, perhaps it says something more significant about how we envisage marriage and parenthood, and why the two seem to get on so badly. Both are badges of adult status, yet the adult worlds they represent, at least in the current state of things, are often profoundly incompatible.

Having children brings our expectations of ourselves as individuals into direct conflict with the reality of our lives as parents, but parenthood means different things for men and women, for mothers and fathers. This is perhaps not the case in general terms, since the vast majority of parents love their children, do their best for them, want the best for them, but it is certainly so in terms of the day-to-day, minute-on-minute experience of parenting, and also, very probably, in terms of the deeper emotional and psychological connections that exist between mothers and fathers and their children. Mothers still spend far more time with their children, and a straightforward outcome of a woman's greater involvement is a degree of familiarity that few fathers can match. Mothers know how many fillings their children have; have many vaccinations they still need; whether their child's best friend was in school that day. Fathers seldom know these things. Some don't want to. For others it is a cause for real regret. In the UK there are now 90,000 at-home dads, all of them familiar with the pros and cons of being 'lead parent'. In the US, 1.9 million fathers of children under 15 are now primary carers, compared to 400,000 in the 1970s.[35] For the majority of families, though, the lead parent is still usually the mother. The sensation of being embedded in our children's lives is one of life's best and worst gifts to parents.

Many women positively thrive on the sense of involvement and intimacy with their children. 'The feeling of loving these two people more than anything, and being loved by them makes it all worthwhile,' says Ruth. 'It's fantastic knowing that there are these two people in your life who just adore you and want to be with you, who are always, always pleased to see you.' Virtually all mothers know the pleasure of this sense of reciprocal loving. But there are many mothers who feel at times enchained by the responsibilities of mothering, burdened as much as privileged, anxious about what is happening to them as they watch their lives become their children's property. Was the novelist Doris Lessing monstrously inhuman when she walked out on her two small children to start a new life on her own, or was she just acting out a familiar fantasy? Was Alison Hargreaves, the mountaineer killed while climbing Everest, irresponsible to undertake such a dangerous activity when she had two young children back at home, or was she perfectly entitled to do what she wanted with her own life regardless of being a mother? And what about Sylvia Plath, committing suicide in the kitchen, with her young children asleep in the next room? Should we condemn her selfishness in putting her own misery before the long-term suffering her death would cause her son and daughter? Or pity her, for succumbing to pressures that in lesser form many of us can recognise from our own lives? 'I know this is just a short phase,' says Fiona, 'I know I'll come out the other end in a few years' time. What I don't know is what will be left of me by then!'

Whatever meanings we ultimately, privately, draw from our experiences of motherhood, whatever the consequences for our relationships with our children, and with our partners, we owe it to ourselves to remember that mothering shouldn't be a short cut to martyrdom. Family life is an extraordinary mix of the mundane and the extraordinary, the rewarding and the demoralising, the intense and the intensive. Much of the task of containing these opposites falls to mothers, maybe it always will; but for ourselves, for our children, for our partners, we need to stay in the frame, not just become the frame.

Our second child represents a particular challenge. With one child, we can just about continue as before, at least on the surface. With two children, the additional pressures on our physical, financial and emotional resources require us to make decisions about how we want to lead our lives. Muddling through doesn't work as well second time round. We all do it, of course, and muddling through is, in one sense, what it's all about. But if all we're doing is muddling through, sooner or later we run into difficulties. Instead, we need to think about how we want to balance our children's needs with our own, our own needs with our partner's, our needs as a family with our needs as a couple, our needs as a couple with our needs as an individual. If we're pulling the same way as our partner, if our expectations for ourselves and our hopes for our children are reasonably well-matched to our abilities and temperaments, if we have evolved ways of coping with problems and disagreements so that they don't overwhelm us or poison daily life, if we can shrug our shoulders about our shortcomings and our partner's shortcomings, and instead focus on what's good about us and them and our life together, if we can still see the thread of our own lives winding its way through the present and on into the future, then we're doing OK, more than OK, we're doing marvellously.

'There is something on your shoulder
which goes beyond family-friendly.'

Seven

BETWEEN A ROCK
AND A WORKPLACE

Before I had children, I imagined – as a good born-and-bred feminist – that I would do my bit for my infants by staying at home and breast-feeding for a few months, then return to full-time work, having installed them in some carefully checked childcare. Children seemed to me to present a practical problem. Not an emotional one. Just a practical one. But from the moment I took my first child to the nursery that she was meant to start full-time the following week, I realised the vast errors in my thinking. I'd been programmed all wrong! I'd had the wrong data input. Now, confronted with the reality of 'high quality childcare provision', for which I'd been an ardent advocate only a week before, the idea of leaving my precious daughter anywhere near it was inconceivable. I back-pedalled. Applied for a part-time place. Called social services for a list of registered childminders. Put up a notice for nanny shares. Anything rather than do what I'd always planned and go back to work full-time.

A month later, I gingerly deposited my seven-month-old baby with a gentle, loving childminder with whom she quickly and strongly bonded. From then on I needn't have worried about her, but I did. I worried that she should have been at home more, that I should have been working less, that I should have been working more, that her father should have been working less to enable the first and the third propositions to be compatible (another fallacy). By the time I got pregnant with my second child, I knew my days of full-time work were gone, if not for good, then at least for the next five years. I had down-shifted my expectations to accommodate the previously unimaginable reality of being a mother, of loving my children, of being needed by my children. I am resigned to working less than I'd like, earning less than I'd like, achieving less than I'd like and doing more housework than I'd like. This compromise involves, paradoxically, doing both more and less mothering than I'd like. It is driven by financial, emotional and practical considerations. On the days I do work, I no longer consider whether or not my children mind my working – I just head for the door as fast as possible. Maybe that means I've at last got 'the balance' right. Whatever that means.

Fifty years ago, the majority of women stopped work when they got married. Twenty years ago, the majority stopped work after they had their first child. Now a new trend is emerging. For a growing number of women today, the first child is no longer the significant factor in determining whether or not we carry on working; for many of us, our *second* child now marks a watershed in our working lives, affecting the hours we work, the reasons why we work, and, most crucially of all, the way we feel about work.

Margaret, 38, was until recently a senior editor in a large publishing company. She always intended to work full-time as well as having children. When her first child was six months old she returned to work full-time. Even before her second child was born, however, she was beginning to wonder if she wanted to continue with her high-level, high-stress job. 'I was much more tired during my second pregnancy, and I was much more adversely affected by the stress at work – the in-fighting, the office politics, all really took it out of me. Once my son was born, I decided to go freelance, so that I'd be more in control of the hours I worked and the pressure I was under. It's a long way from what I expected and planned when I got pregnant again and I expect some people would see it as giving up. I see it as a temporary situation and a positive solution. I imagine I'll want to work full-time for an organisation again in the future, but this is what I want for now, for myself, for the children, and for our family as a whole.'

Margaret thinks that she underestimated the impact that two children would have on her life, not only in terms of energy levels ('I'm much more tired with two – it's that simple!') but also in terms of her values and attitudes towards work. 'I don't want my life to be so dominated by my work while the children are so young. My work is still very important to me, but it occupies a different place in my life. It's less crucial to my sense of who I am. I wonder where this change in me comes from – is it hormonal or biological, or does it come from social pressure? Even if I could earn twice as much my husband – and I was earning more than him before leaving my job – I'm not sure I would want to go back to that, not right now.'

This is a familiar story to Liz Bavidge, former Director of the Women Returners' Network. 'The attitude among women themselves is changing. They don't want to sacrifice their children for their careers, or vice versa. We're hearing a growing sense of entitlement to combine work and children. Most women with small children want a portfolio life. They want to find ways of combining work and family. They want to do something worthwhile with their time, not just earn money.' Bavidge has noticed that the second child often seems to change a woman's perspective on work. 'We receive about 50 calls a week, and it's clear that the issues women want to talk about change for one and two children.

After the first child, women are often going back to work at a similar level to before, and they want advice about how to handle that. But after two children, many women want to change the *balance* of how they work. They want to know how to change their hours, how to change the kind of work they're doing.

With one child, it is possible to combine home life and work. Life gets busier, but it's the slack that is taken up. With two, there isn't any slack and most people find something has to give. With a second child, you find yourself increasingly pulled into the world of small children. There is less time, less energy, more competing claims on your resources. It becomes appreciably more difficult to move between the spheres of home and work.

The Women Returners' Network was set up to provide advice, solutions, ideas, support and information to women returning to the workplace after a period of time out of it. Very often, however, Liz Bavidge and her colleagues found themselves simply giving women permission to do what they wanted to do. 'I had a very high-powered woman ring me last week. She'd recently gone back to work after having her second child and was basically wanting to rethink her whole life. She's earning £120,000 a year and doesn't know if she's allowed to cut back on her work. She wanted permission to do so.'

It says a great deal about the conflicting pressures on women today that it has become so hard for mothers to *know* what they want to do. Ruth, mother of Rachel and Hannah, worked as an architect before her children were born. She went back to part-time work after her first child. 'I didn't really want to go back to work at all, but I felt I ought to. There was a lot of pressure – from other mothers, from my partner, from myself. The whole message seemed to be: you mustn't let children ruin your career; feminism has fought hard for this right; now don't let the side down. By the time I got pregnant with Rachel I had a better sense of what I wanted, and felt more able to make my own choices. I haven't worked regularly since she was born, and that's fine. It's not great being financially dependent on my husband after being used to earning my own money, but otherwise I'm very happy. It's a relief not having to do everything. I'm fairly confident my work will pick up once the girls are both at school and I have more time.'

Other mothers want to carry on working at the same level as before, but find the strain of combining both working and mothering too great.

Charlotte worked as a foreign language teacher up until the birth of her second child. 'I didn't see how I was going to manage two children and a full-time job, so I stopped work completely after Saskia was born. Then I began to feel I ought to be working, earning some money, not just being a housewife! I got another teaching job in a language school, and almost immediately the stress levels in our household went through the roof. Mornings were awful, evenings were awful, weekends were awful. There was never any time to stand still. Our whole life was a rush and it took all the pleasure out of it. I lasted six weeks and then gave up work again. It wasn't something I did for the children, it was for me too. I don't see myself as a housewife, but the fact is that is what I am right now. The girls are six and eight, but they still seem to need me around as much as ever. This isn't how I planned things; it's just how they worked out.'

Charlotte did not make a clear-cut 'choice' about work. Faced with various competing priorities, she tried several different solutions, eventually settling on the one that works best for the moment. It may or may not be temporary. It certainly doesn't reconcile all her priorities. It is simply the best option available for her and for her family at the moment.

Logistics Overload: The True Story

Many women 'drop out' of the world of work after their second child is born, not because of any ideological position on working mothers, but because the practicalities of life with two children just make it too much of a logistical headache.

Fiona was a catering manager before her first child was born, switched to part-time work after he was born, and nine months after her second child was born, stopped working altogether. 'Luke is three now, and Phoebe is in school, but I'm still not working, even though I really want to get back to something. The problem is what kind of something? I have to drive 15 miles to school and back each morning, and I can't find a nursery that fits in with school hours. It's just too difficult to organise. I've resigned myself to waiting until they're both a lot older.'

Childcare arrangements inevitably become more complicated with two children – another of the hidden aspects of life with more than one child. Unless you are in the position to afford a nanny, you will be faced with arranging childcare for two children with very different requirements:

the nursery that is perfect for a three-year-old, may not be the right environment for a six-month-old baby; the nanny who is wonderful with a child under two may have little understanding of the needs and interests of a pre-schooler; a school that may have worked brilliantly for your first child may be quite the wrong place for your second.

The way childcare is discussed in the press you'd never imagine how complicated the reality is, but for the vast majority of mothers who also work, childcare is not a fixed point, but a moving target that requires ingenuity, energy and determination to pin down. Most mothers cobble together the childcare they need out of a mixture of friends, neighbours, grandparents, and what is rather quaintly called 'formal provision', meaning you pay for it. 'It' being nannies, childminders, playgroups and nurseries of hugely varying size, cost and quality. But that is by no means the end of the story, because, once cobbled together, these childcare arrangements will display a remarkable tendency to uncobble again on a regular basis.

Jane's childcare arrangements had worked well with her first child, but broke down with her second child, with direct consequences for her work as a freelance musician. 'Imogen had been with her childminder since she was a baby and had always been very happy there. We assumed that our next child would go there too, but it didn't work out. Jessica didn't settle at all. It was all too noisy and busy for her, and we worried that she wasn't getting enough focused attention. After a couple of months we found a nanny to come and look after her at home. But that gave us a new problem because we couldn't afford to pay a nanny and a childminder, and Imogen was very upset and angry at having to leave her childminder, because she had really grown to love her. In the end I decided the only way was to cut down on my hours to meet the costs. That's been all right for the children, but it has been very frustrating for me, as I've watched work opportunities come up that I haven't been able to respond to.'

For some women it is the *cost* of working that pushes them out of a job: paying childcare for two children, whether full-time or part-time, costs more than they can earn in a week. This is the reason women most often give when asked why they don't work longer hours, or don't work at all. Celia stopped work when her younger child, Frances, was one. 'I had to accept that the finances just weren't working out. Even working part-time, I couldn't afford the childcare. In effect, I was paying to work.'

On paper the costs of childcare don't seem to vary much from one child to two. According to the official figures, a working mother-of-one child spends on average £41 per week, while a working mother-of-two children spends on average £47 per week. These are averages, however, and, in any case, don't take account of the cobbling and de-cobbling that's going on. According to the 1996 Labour Market Trends, three-quarters of working mothers pay nothing for childcare. The costs don't vary much from one child to two on paper, because many women change their childcare arrangements rather than what they spend on childcare. The majority of working mothers find ways of avoiding the increase in the costs of childcare for two children, but the result is that the *logistics* of childcare become even more daunting than they were with one.

Caroline has worked part-time since she had her first child, six years ago. 'But that makes it sound so neat and tidy,' she says with a laugh. 'Whereas, in fact, my working hours have changed from year to year and my childcare has had to change too. I'm actually finding it harder now then when the children were very small. I went back to work four days a week when Thomas was four months old and I had a nanny-share with a friend which worked very well. She left for New Zealand just before I had Bridget. I took six months' maternity leave, found a new nanny, and went back to work three days a week. That lasted for two years, then she left to go travelling too, and at the same time we moved house and Thomas started school. I found a childminder for Bridget, but she didn't drive, so Thomas went home with a friend after school on my working days, which by now had dropped to two and a half days. A month ago the childminder told me she's retiring! Bridget's now in nursery four mornings a week until lunchtime, but that doesn't solve the problem as my work means I have to do whole days. I haven't yet found a regular arrangement for Thomas after school this term either. Honestly! I spend so much of my time trying to organise childcare, if we didn't need the income from my job, I'd be seriously tempted to just pack it in for the next year until they're both in school. But having got this far that seems a bit ridiculous.'

For any mother who relies on a nursery or childminder to care for her offspring while she works, the hourly rates will increase by a third or even double when she has another child. Only the most expensive childcare option of all – a nanny – does not get more expensive with two children, so long as both children stay at home with the nanny. If the older child progresses to a nursery, however, the financial costs soar. Half way through her second pregnancy, Lorraine, a junior account manager for a firm of management consultants, sat down and worked out how her new baby was going to affect her bank balance. 'It's terrifying. I already pay £300 a week for a full-time nanny for my daughter. She starts nursery in the autumn, which is £90 a week, but I'll still need the nanny for the baby, so I'll be paying out £390 a week. That's nearly £20,000 a year! That's a sizeable percentage of my income.'

What women decide to do about work is directly affected by the cost of childcare, but most mothers do not want more childcare so that they can work longer hours; they want more flexibility in their work so that they don't have to have more childcare. According to Professor Alan Marsh at the Policy Studies Institute, women set a ceiling on what they can afford to pay for childcare, regardless of the hours they work or the number of children they have. 'The proportion of income spent on childcare doesn't actually change very much from one child to two, or two to three. The research evidence is notoriously hard to read, but what appears to be happening is that most women cap the amount they'll spend on childcare to about a quarter of their income, and then cut their hours accordingly. While there are some women who will do anything to stay in the labour market and pay for childcare accordingly, most approach the problem from the opposite direction. In other words, the majority of women don't look for the childcare to suit their job, they choose their job to suit their childcare needs, and this is what drives their decisions about work.'

Women budget only once for childcare; after that it is their working hours that must adjust. In Britain, consequently, only one-fifth of working mothers pay more than £80 per week on childcare, and only one-fifth of working mothers work full-time. The government likes to interpret this as meaning that more affordable childcare would keep more women in full-time work. But Professor Marsh, among others, is cautious about interpreting the figures in this way. 'It's very difficult to show that lack of affordable childcare is preventing women from staying in the workplace. Women seem to assess the pros and cons of being at home, and then the pros and cons of being at work, but the two assessments are like parallel seesaws, rather than opposite ends of the same seesaw. When both seesaws tip in the same direction, women choose that option.' It's a complex decision-making process that involves women making complicated judgements about their aggregate quality of life, and as Alan Marsh cautions, 'It is virtually impossible to disentangle the cost of childcare from women's wish to be with their children.'

Ah yes! A woman's wish to be with her children.

It sounds so simple, so obvious. And yet it has become one of the hottest potatoes on offer in contemporary Western society. For in today's world, a woman's wish to be with her children must not interfere with her duty to earn a living (according to the Treasury), nor her professional commitments (according to her employer), not to mention her personal ambitions. There is something wholly bizarre about the situation in which so many mothers find themselves: for every woman justifying her wish not be with her children, there is another having to justify the opposite.

The Myth of Choice

Whether you are working part-time, full-time or not at all, the relationship between work and children becomes appreciably more fraught after you have your second child. A recent survey found that 79 per cent of working mothers were disillusioned with work. Another found that 75 per cent of working mothers said they had no idea before having children how hard it would be to combine work and mothering. It is after having our second child that most of us will find ourselves having to rethink what place work is going to have in our lives, at least for the next few years.

According to Hugh Davies at Birkbeck College, London, the effect of children differs in other countries. 'In some countries, it's the number of children you have that affects whether or not you work; in other countries, it is the age of your youngest child that makes the difference. Britain seems to be moving from age to number. We're observing in our research that more mothers of very young children are in employment, but that mothers with *more* than one young child are less likely to be working.' In other words, the number of children you have is now having more effect on whether or not you are likely to be in paid work of some kind, than the age of your children. This is a massive change from 30 years ago, and one which merits serious attention. It is a shift that reveals a great deal about the reality (as opposed to the ideal, the hype and the pretence) of combining paid work with children, a reality that is physically exhausting, emotionally stressful, financially costly (in the short term) and logistically horrendous.

The triumphalist note to reports that more women are now in paid work than ever before, or that in some parts of the country there are now more women in work than men, is misleading. What these reports gloss over are the telling details. Yes, the number of women working full-time after the birth of their first child is rising, but the proportion of women *still* working full-time after the birth of their *second* child drops dramatically. It is true that most women now work full-time up to the birth of their first child, and it is also true that more women today will return to work afterwards. A mere 20 per cent of women now stop work after the birth of their first child. But most women still do not work full-time when their children are very young. In Britain, the majority of mothers of children under five work part-time, and the majority of part-timers are mothers – four and a half million women in Britain currently work part-time; three and a half million of them are mothers. Of those mothers who do go back to work full-time after the birth of their first child, about one-third later switch to part-time work. 'Later' in most cases means after their *second* child!

In 1996 Dr Katherine Hakim raised a storm in a sociological teacup when she argued in the *British Journal of Sociology* that women make a choice not to be work-oriented when they decide to have children, and that policies aimed at encouraging women into the workplace are a waste of time and money. There was a cry of outrage from feminist sociologists, who attacked Hakim's methodology and analysis. But Hakim was making an important, if unfashionable, point: the great majority of women with small children are 'choosing' not to be work-oriented and don't want to join the workforce to the detriment of their children. Hakim, however, made it sound like a straightforward weighing of the pros and cons.

Often women do not set out to make a rational decision about how many hours they work, but simply end up doing what they're doing for a whole raft of interwoven reasons. Melissa Benn, author of *Madonna and Child*, and herself a mother of two young children, also thinks that Hakim oversimplified. 'Hakim thinks that women give up their ambition when they have children, but it's more complicated than that. Many women find that their ambitions change after having children. I know from my own life that I now have ambitions that include my children. For women who are going along the path of 'having it all', they can usually keep those two parallel worlds of work and children going after their first child. But the second, especially if it is going to be her last, makes her think differently. Having two children's lives to organise alongside your work makes a huge difference. It takes time and commitment and thought. It's not something you can squeeze into a few hours a week. For most women who have the option, the decision to cut back on the hours they work, the decision not to try and 'have it all' is not a cop-out, but a productive and rich, though complicated, choice that reflects their changing perspective and priorities.'

The 'choices' a woman makes about whether or not to work after having children are informed by a complex web of factors – her financial situation, her partner's attitudes, her age, class, social background, education, occupation – and by less obvious, less-documented factors too, such as how well her children sleep at night!

In a landmark book, written in the early 1970s, *The Symmetrical Family*, Michael Young and Peter Wilmott envisaged a future in which men and women would no longer divide work so that women took responsibility for housework and children, while men took responsibility for paid work outside the home. Instead they would adopt more egalitarian roles in which each adult did two jobs, both the man and the woman would do the unpaid work of running a home and bringing up children and the paid work. In a few, exceptional households this has happened. And the result? Both the man and the woman are over-stretched and exhausted. In rather more households, the split is more like three jobs for the woman, and one and a tiny bit (if that) for the man. The real problem for many women is that they are doing their three jobs in the same amount of time they were once expected to do one. The ideal of men and women each doing two jobs falls down badly because the work may have doubled, but the time it takes to do it in has not been halved. The solution for many women with small children – part-time work – brings its own problems. In Britain, however, part-time work still denotes in employer's eyes a decline in commitment to work. For most mothers, though, it is not declining commitment that is the issue, but diminishing time, money and stamina.

A second child creates an exponential rise in the amount of time that must be spent on child-related activities (playing, teaching, cleaning, cooking, washing, shopping), and unless you're in the live-in nanny league, working full-time simply doesn't leave time to do it. Many women who do try to 'do it all' often live, not with a sense of triumph, but with the sense of being spread too thinly. Maria, mother of Lucy and Kate was a barrister until fairly recently. She spent an hour with her children in the morning before the nanny arrived at 8.00am, when she would get herself dressed and leave for work. She arrived home between 7.00pm and 7.30pm and spent half an hour or so with the children before they went to bed. Maria's husband, Gregory, is also a barrister and was working similar hours. The toll of this lifestyle was considerable; Maria felt increasingly anxious about the effect on her children, but couldn't see any way of changing her hours. 'I realised very soon after Lucy was born that it wasn't going to be so simple to combine work and a family. I took four months maternity leave, which I'd thought would be plenty, but when it came to it, I wasn't at all ready to go back to work. I really didn't want to leave her, but my chambers wouldn't let me take any more time so I didn't have much choice. After my second child was born, I was a bit more senior and had a bit more say, and I negotiated a slightly shorter week. The problem didn't really go away though. It's not the kind of work you can regulate in that way – it's very unpredictable. If I was on a big case, I might be working flat out for weeks. If I only took on the little cases, I'd be seen to be not pulling my weight and the clerks would get fed up. I hated seeing so little of the children, and I could hardly bear to think what they felt. But working part-time wasn't really an option. I thought about stopping altogether for a while, but knew how hard it would be to get back in again later. For a long time I just couldn't see a solution. I felt caught either way.' Eventually, Maria and her husband restructured their lives to allow more space for their children's needs. For Maria, this meant deciding to leave work entirely. Her long-term plan is a change of career, to something more family-friendly. In the short-term, she is at home with her girls.

Work and the Second Child Syndrome

In *The Time Bind*, American sociologist Arlie Hochschild reported that many American families are suffering from a 'time deficit'. With both parents in full-time work in these households, there is simply not enough parent to go round. Something has to give, and often, worryingly, it appears to be home life that loses out. Hochschild observed that people were spending more and more time at work, seeking refuge from the impossible task of running a family in too little time. Going home to a neglected spouse, resentful children and a mountain of housework was less appealing than the polite supportiveness of colleagues and the clear-cut aims and rewards of the office.

'For most working mothers with young children,' writes Susan Maushart in *The Mask of Motherhood,* 'life is a juggling act that keeps them too exhausted to examine the quality, let alone the inequality of the experience.'[1] Sarah Jackson of Parents At Work agrees: 'Every woman with two children will say that juggling work and home becomes significantly more difficult after the second child.'

In short, what everyone is beginning to notice is the until now unnamed 'Second Child Syndrome'. Women don't make a one-off decision about the kind of mothers they want to be, the kind of working life they want to have; they revisit the decisions they make, as their feelings and experiences change. Often the catalyst for those changes is the second child. One study found that of those women planning to have another child, 40 per cent had already decided to cut back on work or cut it out altogether once their second child was born.[2] Several of these women had simply not imagined before becoming mothers how much they would love their children, how much they would want to be with them. They saw their second child as the justification they needed to step back from paid employment for a while. Of the women I interviewed, only two carried on working full-time after their second child, and one of those women, Alex, not for long. All the others either reduced their working hours, or stopped work completely. These decisions were not taken lightly; in most cases, they were the result of many factors jostling for supremacy over a period of many months.

One of the most recent, detailed studies of women's working patterns is a longitudinal survey of 400 British women conducted by social psychologists at the University of Kent. The study was designed to find out how attitudes to work and childcare change after the birth of a woman's first child. Dr Diane Houston was particularly interested in how women's intentions and attitudes change after they become mothers, and what they do about it. 'What we found from our data was that the majority of women now intend to go back to work after their first child is born, and that they are *carrying out that intention*, even if their views and feelings about work change once the baby actually arrives.' Diane Houston's research also began to reveal other, unexpected patterns. 'We know from the statistics that the majority of women with pre-school children work part-time, but our research was clearly showing that women were increasingly likely to return to work full-time after the birth of their first child. So that led us to ask: what is happening?' Her survey results were indicating that although a woman's intentions and attitudes to working outside the home might diverge after the birth of the first child, intentions and actions nevertheless stayed in line with one another. Instead, to their surprise, Houston and her colleagues found evidence that it is the *second child* who precipitates a significant change in a woman's intentions.

What is more, this shift is occurring even before the second child is born. 'We weren't intending to study the impact of the second child, but a number of our respondents got pregnant again very quickly, so the follow-up interview at 12 months was taking place when they were already expecting their second child. We found the mothers' attitude towards work was very different during second pregnancy than it had been during first pregnancies. In terms of the choices women make about working outside the home, it is almost certainly the second child that makes the real difference.' As Houston found, becoming pregnant for the second time was enough to trigger a significant change in attitudes and intentions towards work.

For decades women were assured that going out to work, getting out of the house, would solve the problem of 'the captive wife', the depressed mother at home with small children. Well, the majority of women with children do now go out to work, and while it's true that they are less likely to be depressed than mothers who are at home with small children all day, they suffer more from stress and exhaustion and worry more about their children instead. For a great many women, having a second child is what finally tips the seesaws in favour of the family. Even for very career-minded women, the desire to be with one's children, to meet their needs, can start to outweigh the pressure to keep a career in top gear.

In *Ending the Mother War*, Jayne Buxton summarises the complexity of our decision-making with admirable clarity: 'There are many good reasons for a mother to stay home with her children. Because she wants to and can. Because she enjoys spending time with them more than anything else she could be doing. Because, as one mother put it, "it is the biggest privilege imaginable". Because one or more of her children are particularly in need of special care and attention, or because the complex logistics of running a home with three or four children in it go far more smoothly when one parent focuses on attending to them. All of these are positive reasons for being a full-time mother – far more positive than the myth that pretends that a mother must stay home or risk wrecking her marriage and her husband's self-esteem, damaging her children's educational prospects, and turning juvenile delinquents loose upon the world. Far more positive, also, than having to stay home because the only alternative is to work long hours within an inflexible work culture which fails to recognise that children need parents to spend time raising them.'3

The desire to be with our children, however unfashionable, is real and valid. If American employers are winning the battle for mothers, plenty of employers in other countries are scratching their heads at their *failure* to keep women in the workplace despite often generous and imaginative efforts to do so. Is this evidence perhaps that people don't want their children to end up as the guinea pigs in a social experiment in which they never intended taking part?

While life generally gets easier as children get older for women who are at home full- or part-time, women in full-time employment often say that as their children grow older, new needs emerge, new areas of conflict and tension arise, new logistical dilemmas seem to spring up to take the place of the old ones. As Deborah, mother of Caitlin and Zoe, puts it, 'By the time they're four and six, it's not just their clothes and food you're having to think about, but their dental and doctor's appointments, ballet lessons and social lives. If you want to do a half-decent job of it, it takes a lot of time and thought and energy. It is very hard to hand that over to a nursery, or a nanny. It needs to be you.' Emma, mother of eight-year-old Lawrence and six-year-old Annie, has worked full-time since the children were babies, but has now decided to stop work for a while. 'My friends think I'm mad, but what I've found is that the children need me more now than when they were tiny. They don't want to be having tea with a nanny, they want me there, and I think they're right. Their needs are more complicated now and I'm not so easily replaceable as I used to be when they were small.'

Working mothers are juggling incompatible worlds, and those worlds do not become any more compatible as children get older. The working day and the school day are hopelessly ill-matched. In the UK, one in five children aged between five and ten is home alone during school holidays, and one in six goes home to an empty house after school each day. After-school clubs are available to only a fraction of children, as are holiday play-schemes. In any case, we need to ask ourselves serious questions about what kind of life we want our children to be living. Is it really right that our children's day should be endlessly extended to match the adult working day? Isn't this the wrong way round. Some American hospitals now have Lollipop Wards for children too ill to go to school, whose parents don't/can't take time off work to be with them. Hallmark now sells greetings cards with the message, 'I wish I were there to tuck you in' and 'Have a super day at school'.

Employers are less helpful than they could be, as Celia found out when her first child was five. Celia had used a workplace nursery for both her children up until then. 'It worked out very well, because both children were going to the same place for the same number of hours. That's all going to change this autumn, when Frances starts school. Her day will end earlier than mine, and there'll still be Ben to collect from the other side of town. I'm not in the sort of job where I can just leave at 2.45pm, but I can't afford a nanny on top of nursery fees, and in any case, I do feel I ought to collect her from school, at least in her first term or two.' I saw Celia again a few months later. She was relieved to have been granted permission by her employer to leave work early two days a week so that she can pick up her daughter from school during her first term. 'I make up the hours at night, and next term she can go to after-school club. They made it very clear it was a special case.' But why is Celia's a special case? After all it is the situation most parents and school-aged children find themselves in, and Celia can't be the only parent of a school-aged child to work for that company. Why should five-year-old Frances have to go to after-school club, when she's already been at school all day long? Why should Celia have to feel so grateful for being allowed to do two hours' work in the evening? Why can't her employer let her leave early for the next three years or so, not just the next six weeks? Why can't her company make its core hours more family-friendly, say 8.45am–2.45pm not 10.00am–4.00pm?

We are in real danger of infecting our children's lives with our own diseases. British men work the longest hours in Europe and British women aren't far behind. The shift to a 24-hour culture has in some ways helped working parents: we can now shop at Tescos at 3.00am if necessary, in person or on-line. But the inexorable rise of the 24-7 society is another deadly strike at the heart of family life. A survey by the Daycare Trust found that 61 per cent of working families have parents who are obliged to work evenings, nights, early mornings or weekends. These numbers are expected to double in the next six years. Working anti-social hours has become a non-negotiable norm for a substantial number of employees. One in four employed adults in Britain now works between 6.00pm and 6.00am.[4] As a result, a growing number of children seldom or never see their parents simultaneously. This new trend of 'tag-parenting' may overcome some of the problems of combining parenting and paid work, but it leaves no space at all for the needs of children or families.

We are, increasingly, grafting the long-hours culture on to our children's lives. In *Children First*, childcare expert Penelope Leach puts a strong case for rejecting this invidious development. 'Most small children already find the school day stressful; many find the buildings, and the groups within them, uncomfortably large. To those who are only just coping with a short day supported by familiar teachers, a longer day finishing with a different adult must be intolerable… Holidays at school are surely a dismal prospect too, whatever the programme of play activities. Few adults would wish to spend much non-working time in their factories and offices. We all need to escape the tensions of group life, insititutional buildings and the identities we have assumed within them. We all need to come home, relax and be a more private version of ourselves.'[5]

If these problems were faced only by children of school age it would be bad enough, but the fact that they are enountered increasingly by children of five-and-under is more worrying still. While the pro-women branch of the government noisily advocates more nursery provision for under-fives, the concerns of many childcare experts are being drowned out, but as Leach says, 'The public image of daycare is an unrealistically positive one: pre-school children playing and learning together in the playgroups and nursery schools that should indeed be freely available to them all. Less positive and less looked at are images of those same children, seven hours later: past playing, past learning and still with two hours before they are collected. And then there are the images that are seldom seen:

images of babies, a few weeks or a few months old, with nothing to gain from being with other children and much to lose in being left to the care of adults whom they must share… Spending all day in the exclusive company of 20 or more age- and status-peers is stressful for everyone: for adults in open-plan offices as well as for children in school. It is not only extremely stressful but often counter-productive for very young children.'6

Small wonder that so many women pull out of paid work after their first or second child. Small wonder that so many of them decide instead to play the waiting game. 'I'm going to wait until they're both at school'; 'I'll start working again once the younger one's at school'; 'It's only a few years, isn't it?' But is it? The trouble with the waiting game that so many mothers play, is that it gets harder to contemplate re-entering the world of work once you've been steeped in the world of children for five years. Its rhythms, its requirements are so different and so undervalued. Jill is married to an architect and they have two children, aged two and four. She worked as a homeopathic doctor until the birth of her first child. She has decided not to return to work until the children are both at school, even though her work is very important to her. This is not a decision that she made easily, and she is still not sure whether it was the right choice or not. 'I'm sure it is the best decision from the children's point of view, but I'm losing motivation all the time. I find it harder and harder to think about going back to work. It's not just being away from the children, although that does feel very hard still, it's also about how I've changed as a result of being with them for the last three years. I go at a different pace.'

According to Diane Houston's research of 400 mothers, Jill's concerns are very typical of a great many stay-at-home mothers. Before having their first child, all the women in the study were happy that their plans to work or not to work would be the best option for the children and for themselves. One year later, however, women who stayed at home with their children were still very confident that this was right for their children, and rated their children's happiness, security and contentment higher than the mothers who worked, but they were less sure if it was the best thing for them personally. Meanwhile, the women who were combining mothering with full-time or part-time work were much more confident that working was the best thing for them personally, but also much less sure than the stay-at-home mothers about the possible effects on their children. A quarter of the mothers who worked full-time did not think it was the best decision for their children. Three-quarters of all the working mothers had found combining motherhood and work much more difficult than they'd envisaged. They had higher levels of psychological distress than non-working mothers, and 40 per cent planned to reduce their hours or stop work altogether when they had their second child. Many cited the problems of broken nights, illness, childcare costs and the general toll of juggling.[7]

To survive life with small children, you have to lower your expectations of what you can get done, you have to cope with constant interruptions, you have to let go of a goal-oriented approach to the week, the day, the hour, the next five minutes, you have to be reactive, rather than proactive, you have to be flexible rather than focused, you have to be fantastically well organised, but also open to the unexpected. Above all, you have to blur the boundaries of your self to cope with these constant intrusions, incursions and invasions of your thoughts and feelings without going completely insane. For many women, this process also involves a loss of confidence in their ability to cope with the world of work. You don't get out of the house, your social horizons become very restricted, you may go all day without talking to an adult, and the result is that you lose confidence. It is such a central thing, and such an obvious thing, but every woman thinks she's the only one it is happening to. For the women who are feeling that, it feels insurmountable. When you're spending all day with small children, becoming immersed in the minutiae of their daily needs, you move on to their wavelength to survive; you get out of the habit, as Liz Bavidge puts it, of 'joined-up speaking'.

Returning to work, full-time or part-time, has some clear benefits. Robert Stewart found among his American second-time mothers that 'the highest levels of stress associated with such factors as depression, social isolation, and marital difficulties were experienced either by traditional homemakers or by formerly employed women who had not yet returned to their jobs by the four-month post-partum session. Other studies, however, have found that, compared with stay-at-home mothers, women who were combining motherhood with full-time or part-time work had higher levels of psychological distress, and were more likely to be tired, stressed and dissatisfied with their relationships.[8] Of the women I interviewed, those who worked the longest hours often mentioned the strains of combining work and mothering, the stress on their relationships of trying to 'job-share life', as one mother put it, and their concerns about how much was too much for their children, but they were the least likely to experience their children's needs as oppressive. Buffered from small children's demands simply by not being there, they relished the time they did have with their children and tended to have more positive feelings overall about life with young children.

Many professional women are reluctant to be seen to be slowing down the pace of life as a result of the impact of small children – they see it as copping out, or worry that other people will see it that way; they feel they are reneging on their feminist ideals; or throwing away the professional status they have gained through years of hard work.

Professional down-shifting is an admission of failure for many women, however we try to gloss it as a positive choice. But as Penelope Leach points out, this is a reflection on just how low society places children in its priority list. Inflexible hours, little control over hours, long hours – all three stand in the way of women with small children. What most women want is more flexibility in the workplace, so that they can work for the hours that they personally feel are appropriate to their family situations. What most women want is government policies that emphasise and encourage flexibility, rather than lay down prescriptions. What would help women and children and men and families is a concerted challenge to the long-hours culture; more accessible training courses; a more positive attitude from employers towards flexible hours and part-time work; more recognition of the needs of children; more recognition of children as a collective, social responsibility, not just a private, individual one.

It may well be that the quest for cheap childcare and universal employment is a major red herring, a contemporary obsession among policy-makers and politicians that takes no account of the realities of life with small children – of their ongoing, changing, accumulating needs – emotional, physical, psychological, educational, social, medical – needs that can't always be met by proxy parents or even the most caring of grandparents, needs that require parents to parent. This need not stand as an insurmountable obstacle to women working, but it is crazy that it should be so consistently ignored as a real factor in women's decision-making about work.

The Art of Time-Stretching

Most of us are all too familiar with the sensation of running against the clock, of being pulled in different directions, of not having enough time to do everything that needs doing. Here's how to make daily domestic life feel a little longer and a little calmer.

* Spend 'planning time' with your partner, to organise diaries for the week ahead and arrange who can do childcare, shopping, cooking etc.

* Menu-planning for the whole week in advance takes a lot of the pressure off weekday mealtimes.

* Don't overload yourself. Ask friends and relatives if they can help you to balance time – for example by sharing school runs and childcare.

* Try to make specific family time which cannot be cancelled, such as all going swimming together on a Sunday, or having a family meal together once a week.

* Weekday mornings are often stressful and chaotic. Plan as much as possible the night before: get clothes ready, organise packed lunches, school bags etc.

* Use star-charts to encourage the children to get up/ get dressed/ eat breakfast in the morning. The domestic rush hour is much easier when everyone's pulling together.

* Involve your whole family in chores and meal preparation – it makes it a family event and shares the load. Let children plan some of the meals right through from shopping to serving.

* Try going to bed 15 minutes earlier and getting up 15 minutes earlier – you'll feel less like you are against the clock in the morning and more in control.

(Adapted from 'Parents' Week Top Tips For Juggling Time', The National Family and Parenting Institute, October 2000.)

Taking the 'Ug' Out of Juggling

Most mothers make short-term strategies aimed at damage limitation and personal survival. They justify and rationalise them in socially acceptable terms: their children's needs or the cost of childcare. The truth is that women love their children, care about their welfare, want to spend time with them, need time away from them, don't want to forego everything they may have achieved before them, and want to find some way of combining work and children that allows for all these facts and enables them to stay sane and have enough energy to say 'Hello' to their partners in the evening.

Know Your Rights

● MATERNITY LEAVE: all pregnant employees are entitled to 18 weeks leave from work, regardless of length of service; most women are entitled to Statutory Maternity Pay or Maternity Allowance during this period, as well as all their usual terms and conditions of employment; if you have worked for your employer for one year or more, you can take a further 29 weeks off work; taking time off work for maternity leave does not affect your right to paid annual leave under the Working Time Regulations; if your employer can't give you back your original job on your return to work, you must be offered an appropriate alternative with equivalent terms and pay as in your previous position; if you think you have been dismissed or disadvantaged at work for any reason connected to your pregnancy, childbirth or leave from work, you can complain to an employment tribunal.

● PARENTAL LEAVE: you are allowed a total of 13 weeks unpaid leave if you have been in your current job for a year or more; with multiple births, you can take three weeks off per child; your contract will continue through your absence; you can return to your old job if you are off for four weeks or less; if off work for more than four weeks, you can return to your old job or, if that's not possible, to an appropriate new one; your employer can postpone your leave for up to six months if they feel your absence would disrupt business unduly, but not if the time off you want starts immediately after the birth of your baby; if your leave is postponed, your employer must tell you why, specify the dates you can take, and give notice of the delay not more than seven days after you say you want time off; if you think your leave is being postponed unfairly, you can bring a claim at an industrial tribunal.

● TIME OFF FOR DEPENDENTS: in addition to the above, all employees are entitled to leave from work to care for dependents (including children) in the event of a genuine emergency without being dismissed for doing so. This includes: unexpected illness or injury; unexpected breakdown in care arrangements of a dependent –a childminder fails to turn up for example; unexpected closure of school, or unavoidable reason for child not attending school. There is no limit to the amount of time taken for emergency care, and no limit to the number of times this kind of leave can be taken.

If government policy were focused on phases rather than issues, there might be a chance of achieving the flexibility that parents want and need from the workplace. Instead of seeing it as a childcare issue, it would be more constructive to look at the ways in which childcare needs change for parents and for children. A mother of a three-month-old baby will suffer if she has to put her infant in full-time childcare in order to keep her job. Her child may well suffer too. Nurseries may be fine for a three-year-old but the wrong environment for a tiny baby. A mother of a four-year-old will be happy to see her child in some kind of group care, confident he is as ready for it as she is. A nursery that runs until only 11.30am, however, creates more problems than it solves if she is employed – children of working mothers are effectively disadvantaged in this way by having to attend nurseries that are not attached to schools. And once children are at school, there is the mismatch between the school day and the working day.

We want to show our commitment to work, for personal, financial and political reasons, but we also have commitments to our children – women still take most of the responsibility for these commitments, because flexibility in the workplace is even harder for men to achieve. The current trend to create more and more childcare without increasing flexibility for either men or women does little to solve the real problem, it just increases the pressures on parents to make choices between their working life and their families. It is entirely appropriate – may even prove to be crucial – for parents to spend time with their children, for children to spend time in their homes with their parents – when they are very young. It shouldn't be about parents chosing, but about employers accommodating.

Women do want to work, but most of them don't want to work full-time when their children are small. Or perhaps it is that they don't want or can't afford full-time childcare, and therefore have no option but to cut back on work. Eighty per cent of Britain's six million part-time workers are women. The government bemoans the lack of family values, the decline of family life, the rise in under-age pregnancies, the juvenile crime rate, but what does it expect in a society where children's lives are increasingly divorced from those of their parents; where children, too, leave the house from 8.00am until 6.00pm and see their parents for only an hour or two in the evening? What scope for family cohesion with so little value placed on family time? It is often said that children grow up too fast 'nowadays', but perhaps they do so in response to the many messages we give them that contemporary society has little space or time for childhood.

To work or not to work has become a big issue for women at all social levels. We work for company, for money, for independence, for time away from children and housework, for our mothers, for our daughters, for ourselves. For the poorest women, the kinds of work available may mean anti-social hours for rates of pay that don't cover the cost of decent childcare. Taking on paid work may mean losing out on valuable benefits, or cheating the system. Single mothers – who are also among the poorest women – are increasingly under pressure to go out to work, even though they are the ones with least slack at all in their lives. No wonder they feel put upon. At the other end of the ecnomic scale, professional women regard work as an integral part of adult life in the way that men do. Above all, work is a right, fought for and earned by a century of feminism.

The paradox at the heart of the feminist achievement is that while it has hugely expanded the scope of women's lives, it has failed to take on board what is still the central experience in most women's lives – mothering. Feminism has never really got to grips with motherhood – other than to suggest that children should be regarded as a logistical complication, easily solved by increasing childcare provision. Mothering has long been regarded by feminists with suspicion bordering at times on bitterness and loathing: children ruin your life, reduce you to domestic slaves, wreck your professional credibility, numb your brain, dry up your sex drive, undermine your efficiency in the workplace (though, God knows, you have to be pretty efficient to get there in the first place once you've got children) – that's the message that feminism has drummed into our heads for several decades now. 'Running through the women's liberation movement has been a thread of hostility to mothers and babies,' writes Ann Dally in *Inventing Motherhood*. 'Lip service is paid to them, but the effect is often the feeling that they are really rather a nuisance, obstruct the correct scheme of things and should be controlled and disposed of as quietly as possible.'[9]

With this contradiction at its heart, feminism has set impossible standards for mothers. As Maureen Freely puts it, in *What About Us? An Open Letter to the Mothers Feminism Forgot*, trying to use the theories of feminism in our daily lives is like 'trying to perform open-heart surgery on [oneself] with a wrench and a crowbar'.[10] Instead of getting to grips with motherhood, feminism has avoided it, denigrated it, urged against it, or simply ignored it. The huge persistent fact of it has still not been adequately confronted, and as a result mothers who are also feminists continue to live with feminism's inherent contradiction. 'Once I knew exactly how to change the world,' writes Freely, 'Now I just get through the day. And the most taxing part of it all is not feeding the children or clothing the children or even finding the time and space in which to work. It's the interior monologue, which, if I transcribed it, would read like a woman's page run amok. I can't walk from one end of my kitchen to the other without querying my motives or comparing myself unfavourably with two warring tribes of ideal types.'[11]

Our emotional, physical and psychological resources are not infinite. Our second child creates a significant additional call on those resources. Many women choose to reduce their work commitments for a while when children are very young because they calculate that there are not enough of these resources to go round satisfactorily at this stage of their lives. With one child you can manage the two worlds, you can live up to your expectations of yourself, or you can at least conceal your concerns that those expectations are no longer so relevant as they were before you had a child. With two children, it becomes far harder to do either. It is harder to pretend your children aren't missing out. It is harder to pretend there's time for your partner. It is harder to survive yourself without something giving.

'The problem that has no name for today's mothers is the struggle to reconcile the rhetoric of equal opportunity with the stubbornly unequal realities of family life,' writes Susan Maushart[12] – and she surely has a point. Melissa Benn thinks there are encouraging signs that motherhood – after so long in the cold – is being recognised as a worthwhile and valuable undertaking. 'I think the ideology is changing: women have more realistic ideas about what they can have and what they can do. They're not berating themselves for not being superwomen.' However we decide to balance children and work, whether the balance feels comfortable or uncomfortable, satisfying or frustrating, the realities of life with small children can only be made easier by more honestly acknowledging and discussing the issues and conflicts that come with modern motherhood. 'Female primates have always been dual-career mothers, forced to compromise between maternal and infant needs,' writes Sarah Blaffer Hrdy in *Mother Nature*. 'It is precisely for this reason that primate mothers, including human foragers, have always shared care of offspring with others – when it was feasible.'[13] For feminism to be antagonistic towards mothers is as crazy as it is for employers to be antagonistic towards children: employers need parents. When women want to work *and* mother, as increasingly it seems they do, then, as Maureen Freely says, 'The only way forward is to speak about motherhood publicly.' And to put fatherhood on the map too.

'Having time together is an absolutely vital precondition for building personal, intimate and supportive relations,' writes Anthony Clare in *On Men*. 'Yet virtually all the trends at the heart of modern capitalism are in the opposite direction... But there is another possibility. Men could join with women to reassert and revitalise a system of values in which the personal, the intimate and the social take precedence over the pursuit of power and the generation of wealth.'[14]

What does this mean in practice? Survey after survey shows that parents want 'family-friendly' workplaces, but as Suzanne Franks, author of *Having None of It*, says, 'If "family-friendly" translates into mother-friendly working it will be meaningless... In that case family-friendly working is simply offering the individual woman a private solution to rearrange her burdens.'[15] All the working mothers I have ever spoken to have understood precisely what Franks means by 'a private solution', and the problems it causes, along with any it may solve. When employers and politicians introduce measures to help women fit mothering around work (or work around mothering), without changing the fundamental organisation of the workplace, it is like a waiter offering a dissatisfied diner a new knife and fork when they've complained about the quality of the food. More childcare being the knife and flexi-time the fork. Thanks a bunch, guys! Very helpful.

Family life remains stoically at the top of parents' priorities, as survey after survey shows, but for that commitment to be realised more easily in our daily lives, we need fundamental changes to take place, both practically and ideologically, in terms of what we do, and how we think.

As well as pushing for change ourselves, we need a government that will put its money where its mouth is: by introducing statutory paternity leave; by improving the rights of part-time workers; by supporting families however they decide to raise their children, neither forcing them into work nor forcing them out of it; by extending statutory maternity leave from its currently sadistic 18 weeks (a number clearly arrived at by someone who'd never given birth, and probably had never been near a baby); by introducing a generous level of parental leave to all parents of children under five; by tailoring the working day to the school day, not the other way round.

We need employers who will get behind flexible working structures for men *and* women; who support fathers who, as Maureen Freely puts it, 'might want to spend less than 25 hours a day at a desk and more than two minutes a week with their children';[16] who endorse rather than penalise a parent's commitments to his or her family; who recognise children as a collective good, not a private problem. We need work structures that make proper allowance for children being born or being ill; that take account of how children's needs change as they grow from infancy to adolesence; that make serious attempts to accommodate the school day and school term; that make real allowance for the importance of fathers as well as mothers in children's lives. We need fathers who stand up to the long hours culture; who don't get going when the family going gets tough; who do their turn on the playgroup rota; who get involved in their local schools. And of course women who feel able to speak publicly, as Freely says, about the experience of motherhood, without fear of reprisal, derision or even just blank incomprehension; who can work out for themselves and their families the best balance of work and parenting, in view of their own particular circumstances, and who can do so openly, honestly and with pride.

For change to be lasting and far-reaching, we need a radical rethink of how we structure time generally. The obsession with 'quality time' has been largely discredited; no one believes any more – if they ever really did – that 15 minutes of concentrated parental attention can achieve the same degree of intimacy as large, formless chunks of time in which parents and children move from attention to inattention and back, available to respond to problems, to be spontaneous, to be quite simply there. Quality time was never going to be an adequate solution when the fundamental problem was lack of time. Children always knew that, parents probably did too. All family time needs to be quality time; the question no one can yet answer is how much is enough.

Work time too needs drastically rethinking, not just how we structure what happens at work, but how we regard work itself. To be more specific, what is needed is a wholesale shift from an age-based approach to time to

Making Work Work

● RESTRUCTURE. Shaping work to accommodate family life is still not as easy as it could be, but there are a range of options that are becoming acceptable to employers, such as flexi-time, part-time work, term-time working, annual hours, employment breaks, job-sharing and home working. Knowing what your options are can help you work out what you need, and for how long. The organisation Parents At Work publishes a *Guide to Flexible Working* that sets out the possibilities. It also gives advice on how to achieve them. In addition, Opportunity 2000, New Ways to Work and The Industrial Society all give advice on working options, employment rights and strategies for securing more compatible working structures. (*See* Help & Advice, p.214.)

● SUPPORT FAMILY-FRIENDLY EMPLOYERS. How? By working for them. This is not always possible of course, but a growing number of firms are committed to family-friendly practice. A number of companies are showing in practical and imaginative ways that they value, respect and support their employees' commitments to their families: Asda, Listawood, IBM, Xerox and Lloyds TSB, to name five shining examples. Public sector employers, too, such as the Royal Borough of Kingston and Oxfordshire County Council, are fostering family-friendly practice. If all these employers can help, why not all employers? Opportunity 2000 and Parents At Work publish directories of family-friendly firms.

● TAKE CONTROL. More and more people are opting to be their own boss. Women in particular are chosing to be self-employed. Independence and flexiblity are the advantages; the drawbacks are isolation, responsibility, cash-flow and workload.

● BE UPFRONT AND VOCAL. Talking honestly and openly about the problems of combining work and family contributes to the groundswell of opinion that families matter and should never be the cause of children suffering.

a phase-of-life-based approach. Ever since the Industrial Revolution, 200 odd years ago, we have acquired the habit of seeing time in terms of work-time versus home-time. It is a habit we seem to be having great trouble shaking off, although for most people today it is increasingly irrelevant and unhelpful. Simultaneously, seeing employment as a constant activity that starts as soon as we leave education and continues until we retire, some 50 years later, is a ludicrous anachronism. Both of these ideas are breaking down under the strain of reality, but they still dominate the way time and work are organised. But as long as policy-makers continue to structure employment around these preconceptions, work will inevitably clash with the needs of families, parents and children. Instead, politicians, employers and employees alike would do better to frame time, both short- and long-term, as a series of overlapping age-bands, each with its own distinctive requirements. We need to be thinking not 'How can I cram all of these things into this amount of time?', but 'How do I need to apportion my time at this stage in my life?' People's needs change at different phases of their lives. It's obvious, isn't it? So why is there currently no differentiation between the needs of a single childless worker in his or her twenties, a married or cohabiting adult with young children in his or her thirties, a single parent with teenagers in his or her forties, and a man or woman in his or her sixties who has plenty of time, but perhaps less energy and poorer health than two decades before.

This weekend my family has been visited by a British Gas engineer in his early thirties, who was working his 14th day in a row, including evening and night shifts, and who'd hardly seen his two children in this past fortnight; by my 28-year-old sister and her husband, who work long hours in the week, but whose weekends and evenings are entirely their own; by my 64-year-old aunt who stopped work last year due to ill health and is now kicking her heels, with far too much time on her hands; and lastly, by my 66-year-old mother, who officially retired last year from her job as an academic, but still clocks up an average of 30 hours a week, sitting on committees, overseeing research programmes, giving lectures and so forth.

Children's needs don't feature anywhere in the consideration of any of these people's employers. For some of our visitors this weekend that doesn't matter yet; for some, it doesn't matter any more; for some it is absolutely crucial. As employees, however, we all fall into just two categories – working or non-working adults.

For 20 years or so in the middle of the average employee's four or five decades of work, children's needs will be a pressing concern, and absolutely *should* be a pressing concern or what kind of parents are we, what kind of adults will our children become? If we want to rise above the undignified, often painful conflict, of 'work versus family', the way that we think about time generally, and working time in particular, has to change.

Eight

PERFECTING IMPERFECTION

'When I grow up, I'd like to be a mummy, just like you,' my daughter announced one morning a few months ago. 'You would?' I said, surprised, having been a less-than-model mother that morning. 'Yes,' she said, in her most grown-up voice, 'it seems very interstressting.'

Inter-*stress*-ting. Precisely!

Every parent at some time or other has trouble with the 'stress' part of life with children, and the early years are for many the hardest. When I had just one child in my life, I felt that on the whole I was the kind of mother I wanted to be – energetic, resourceful, responsive, patient. Becoming the mother of two children turned me into the kind of mother I always intended *not* to be – impatient, distracted, unimaginative, tired, prone to snapping 'in a moment' and 'just wait' and 'not right now' in a tone of voice no one could feel proud of. With two children in my life, I suddenly seemed to spend a far greater proportion of my time doing housework while they watched/played/wandered off somewhere. To be honest, there were times when I preferred housework, because at least I knew what was going to happen next. Arts and crafts and cooking went out the window with my second child – anything with glue or paint or chocolate was, for several years, way beyond my mess threshold – and I have long since lost sight of the charm of being accompanied to the loo. None of this seemed to bother my children nearly as much as I thought it should. But it was an awful shock to me.

Almost imperceptibly, though, life with small children gets easier. One day you realise that your older child has put her coat on without being asked ten times, and without any help from you. Furthermore, she is now standing patiently by the front door while you scurry round the house gathering up nappies, bottles, gloves and wellies. There was a time when that same adorable child would have seized her opportunity to slip into her fairy outfit, or start an elaborate game with the playpeople, or pull out a book she absolutely had to have read to her now. Similarly, a day will arrive when you find yourself walking along the street/out of the door/to the car with both arms miraculously free, because your offspring have reached an age when they can both safely convey themselves along a pavement and into a car. A day will come when you no longer have to approach the weekly supermarket shop like a ground offensive, with a top secret mission to accomplish before the enemy detects what you're up to.

No one will decide to play hide and seek in the aisles. No one will eat the biscuits in the trolley while you're not looking, or leave a careful trail of crumbs in case the witch from *Hansel and Gretel* turns up, to the disgust of the store manager and all the pensioners. Most amazing of all, no one will have a tantrum at the check-out. A day will come when you no longer have to wrench your back hoisting two stone of child into his car seat, nor crick your neck trying to do up the seat belt around your four-year-old (and you thought booster seats would be an improvement!). A day will come when your children accompany you through the world in an orderly fashion. They will wait by shop counters, resist the urge to taste the sweets, manhandle the chocolate, run into the store room, dart out of the door. A day will come when you will be able to buy a paper, or a pint of milk, without impersonating a sufferer of Tourette's syndrome; when you will be able to go to cafés together, without worrying about the people on the next table whose afternoon you are ruining. However hard it is to believe it right now, there will come a day when you will be one of those people yourself, and someone else's children will be ruining *your* afternoon.

You will, in short, find you have emerged from the tempest of early childhood into the lull before the storm of adolescence. Savour every second!

'No one has yet produced a convincing blueprint for perfect parenthood,' observes Christina Hardyment at the end of her book, *Perfect Parents*,[1] a survey of two centuries of changing childcare advice, and these are important words to bear in mind. Parents today, and mothers in particular, bring great anxiety to the job of parenting and at the same time set themselves very high standards. Instead of aiming so high, both we and our children might benefit from lowering our standards at times, expecting less of them and less of ourselves. My first child was treated to a running narrative of her life and mine: Look! Here's a potato, isn't is a funny shape. It's a colour called brown. Can you say brown? B-r-o-w-n. We can do all sorts of things with potatoes – (breaking into song) – bake them, boil them, mash them, fry them…' My second child and I, by contrast, enjoyed long meaningful silences until he was old enough and articulate enough to insist on conversation. Funnily enough, he still learned to talk. When a father I know plucked up courage to switch off his children's cassette of *Winnie the Pooh* and instead put his own tape into the car stereo system, he braced himself for howls of protest from the back seat; instead, after five minutes of *The Dead* by James Joyce, both children fell fast asleep and didn't bother waking up again until they were safely back home.

Imperfect-but-perfectly-adequate parents accept their limitations, or rather they *respect* them. They know it's OK to sit down and ignore their children for minutes at a time; they know that skipping hair washing this week won't cause permanent damage; they don't equate the tidiness of their home with their worth as a parent; they understand that children's clothes don't need ironing; they realise that apple chunks and raisins are wonderful, but there are days when only crisps and chocolate will do. With two children, even more than with one, we all need to accept and respect our limitations. We need to aim for good moments rather than good days. (Good moments are when both children are engaged in an activity that a) isn't too messy; b) isn't too noisy; c) isn't too destructive; d) isn't likely to provoke a fight; e) leaves you free long enough to wash up/cook lunch/put the wet towels in the tumble drier.) Decide right now that you will stop berating yourself for not having got the photos into albums; decide right now that you will save photo albums for your retirement. As Vicki Iovine so rightly observed: 'First-borns have beautiful baby books with written observations, reflections and milestones… By my third baby, I just found a big hatbox and threw everything into it. Who has time to compose diary entries about "Mummy's Dreams for Your Future" when mummy isn't sleeping enough to dream about anything these days?'[2]

Towards the end of his life, Bruno Bettelheim, one of the 20th-century's pre-eminent authorities on child psychology, published a book in which he cautioned against the tendency of modern parents to bow to experts like himself on the matter of bringing up children. Instead, Bettelheim pointed out that family life can never be entirely harmonious and fulfilling: 'Perfectionism is not within the grasp of ordinary beings. Efforts to maintain it typically interfere with that lenient response to the imperfections of others, including those of one's child, that alone make good human relations possible.'[3] At the end of his life, Bettelheim abandoned the idea of ideal parenting in favour of the idea of 'good enough' parenting. We can't be perfect, we don't need to be perfect; what we can do is aim to be good enough.

While many of us would benefit from lowering our expectations of ourselves as parents, we would benefit equally from pushing our needs as adults rather higher up our list of priorities. The physical and emotional demands of looking after two small children – what Helen Simpson so aptly calls 'the ricochet work' – make it more difficult but even more important that we look after ourselves. No one would deny that mothering requires from us a large dose of selflessness, but a bit of maternal selfishness can be far better for our children than worn-out saintliness. Quite apart from the benefits to ourselves, when we show our children that we value and care for ourselves, we are modelling attitudes and behaviour that we hope they in turn will learn and benefit from. Taking time to look after our own needs is good for us and good for them. The consequences of not doing so are significant. Stress, be it emotional, psychological or physical, depresses the immune system, makes us more prone to physical and mental ill-health, and can eventually cause significant physical and emotional problems ranging from long-term back trouble to depression.

Physical exercise is known to be one of the best ways of combatting stress, but unfortunately one of the central paradoxes of life with small children is that you run around all day yet never get any real exercise. All that bending down and picking up and fetching and carrying and moving and sorting – it's downright exhausting, but it doesn't bring any of the usual benefits of physical exertion. Sleep is often in equally short supply at this stage of life, yet lack of sleep is not just miserable, it is debilitating. Losing even an hour or two of sleep a night has a direct toll on our sense of well-being, reducing intelligence, physical co-ordination and problem-solving abilities. Lack of sleep also disrupts our appetite controls and can cause depression. A few years ago I met a man whose wife had died in very tragic circumstances, leaving him with two young daughters to bring up. He'd been suffering from insomnia, which he assumed was caused by the emotional trauma of her death. The problem got so bad he eventually went to his doctor, expecting to be given medication. Instead his GP enquired how long he'd had his present duvet. 'Fifteen years,' he replied, whereupon she suggested he invest in a new one and solve at least one of his problems. He did, and it did.

After the balmy, yet unappreciated days before offspring, we needed time to adjust to the birth of our first child; similarly, after the relative simplicity of having just one child, we need time to adjust to the perpetual (and often also delightful) havoc of life with two. The extent to which this adjustment happens by stealth under our very noses, was brought home to me by a small but telling incident. When my first child was nine months old she developed – as nine-month-olds will – a fascination for telephones. We duly bought her one of those toy phones with flashing lights and twiddly bits that play 13 different tunes when you twiddle them. The problem was that these tunes were unbearably, deafeningly loud. Feeling mean but resolute I took out the batteries. It wasn't until this toy phone resurfaced three years later, when my younger child reached nine months, that my daughter realised she'd been cheated of her 13 tunes and insisted on batteries being installed without further delay. Well now! Either batteries aren't what they were, or my hearing's been shot to pieces, but second time round that little phone plays the gentlest, tinkliest tunes you could imagine.

Like little green frogs in big vats of water, we parents hardly notice the temperature rising around us. Like it or not, it's one of Mother Nature's better strategies for helping us survive being boiled alive! There are other, more attractive options:

Maureen: 'Take up a hobby. Three days after my second child was born I enrolled on a course to learn how to make stained glass. All my friends thought I was crazy. Even I wasn't sure how I was going to get out two nights a week with two children under three. In fact it was the very best thing I could have done. It gave me a goal and a sense of achievement. I'd paid up front for the course, so it also gave me a real incentive to get out of the house. It might seem an odd time to take up a new hobby, but it kept me sane.'

Jane: 'My advice is to throw out the digital clock. When you're being woken at night by two children, it's no help to be able to count the seconds between their night-time wakings. I used to lie there watching the minutes pass, watching my chances of sleep disappear. Knowing I'd only been asleep for 14 minutes and 22 seconds only made it worse!'

Ruth: 'Even if you've chosen to stay at home with the children, you still need some time off. It's absolutely essential. I paid someone to come in twice a week just for one hour between five and six. It let me off the teatime routine and meant I was in a much better mood at bedtime. It really helped. Even if you can't afford to pay someone, you need a break. I'd advocate asking a relative to take one or other of the children off for the day or afternoon on as regular a basis as possible.'

Deborah: 'You can be very isolated when the children are small. It's so hard to get out with a baby and a toddler, and there's never any time to phone other people and make plans to meet up. I used to find days had gone past without my talking to another adult. It took a while to realise that part of the reason I was feeling so low was because I was lonely. My advice to any new mother is to make a point of seeing, or at least talking to other people every day.'

Fiona: 'If you need help, get it now, don't leave it until next week. I think second-time mothers are very hard on themselves: they think they should be coping fine, and they don't want to admit it to anyone if they're not. But if you've got a difficult baby, or a demanding toddler and you're feeling depressed and overwhelmed, it doesn't help any of you to pretend you're managing fine. If you're having problems, talk to your GP, talk to your health visitor – that's what they're there for.'

Joanna: 'What really helped me was when my daughter got to the age when she wanted to go and play at friends' houses. After looking after two children, having just one child seemed so easy – almost as good as being on my own! – and I enjoyed having the time to concentrate properly on the little one. My advice would be: don't feel bad about sending them out to play: it's more fun for them and more restful for you.'

Margaret: 'My children were very close in age, and I was very worried about how I was going to cope when the new baby was very small. My mother lives at the other end of the country, so she wasn't in a position to help after the first couple of weeks. Instead I arranged for my son's childminder to increase his hours, so that he was in full-time childcare while I was on maternity leave for the first six months. I was alone with the baby during the day, and then able to concentrate on my son in the evening when my husband was home from work. It worked very well. I seldom had to manage both of them at the same time, which meant both my son and I could adjust gradually to the new baby. It was fairer and easier for all of us.'

Ruth: 'I took my older child out of nursery when my second was born, so that we were all together while I was on maternity leave. It was a very close, bonding time for our family. The children have a very good relationship now, and I'm sure it was because they spent so much time together when they were tiny.'

Laura: 'Get as much help as you possibly can in the first two months. If you can afford it, I'd really recommend a maternity nurse – it means you can catch up on some sleep and recover from the labour. I had a home help who came in three times a week to do the shopping, cooking and washing for the first month. Coping with the baby and my four-year-old was all I could manage, so the home help made a huge difference. It was nice to have another adult around the house too, for moral support!'

Mary: 'As soon as you have more than one child you have to be organised. I have systems now, where I never bothered before. The toys have places where they live and on a Sunday night I make sure they all go back where they belong. I make sure the children's shoes are put in their rooms at bedtime so I know where to find them in the morning. On the other hand, I try not to be obsessive about it. I never want the house to become a trap. I've seen that happen to too many other women. I never want to feel that there's a cupboard I must tidy before I can sit down and read a book.'

Deborah: 'Weekends are very stressful. You're all home. You're all tired after the week. There's a feeling you should all be doing things together as a family. But when you try, it usually goes horribly wrong. By a process of trial and error, we've slowly learnt that what works best at the weekends is to split up – one of us takes the younger one shopping, the other stays and does something with the older one.'

Margaret: 'I found going swimming twice a week made me feel much more positive and energetic, more able to cope with daily life.'

Joanna: 'My marriage deteriorated dramatically in the year after our second child was born. We'd got as far as talking about splitting up. A friend suggested we join a dance class that she'd been going to with her husband, and it was completely brilliant. Making time every week to do something really fun together got us through a very tough patch.'

Charlotte: 'Don't forget your husband. I've seen a lot of relationships founder after the second child comes along because the woman's up to her eyes and the man feels totally pushed out. My advice to any woman with two small children is book a weekly babysitter.'

Caroline: 'At the time it's so all-consuming. You think the bad bits are going to go on forever. But in fact it's just a phase, and once it's over, you forget about it. My advice to second-time mothers when things are hard is just to keep on reminding yourself that it won't last forever.'

It is amazing what we do eventually get used to in the way of noise, mess, lack of time and lack of sleep. Ultimately it is a matter of finding a balance to your life that suits you personally. For my friend Rachel the key to survival is a strategic mix of self-discipline and self-indulgence: 'How do I survive?' she asks. 'Routine. Going back to work. A daily cappuccino. And nice underwear.'

From a purely rational point of view, it might seem to make more sense to jettison the fantasy family, stick with the manageable model, and stop at one. There is no convincing evidence that being sibling-less is bad for your child, and plenty of convincing evidence that the fewer children you have, the better it is for your bank balance, your marriage, your health, and your promotion prospects. Perhaps these arguments against having more than one child are beginning to sink in; the latest figures from the Office For National Statistics show that the number of lone-child families are growing fast. The norm, however, is still two.

For some people, having two children will be part of the game plan for their life. For others, children may fulfil a need to love, or to be loved. A great many women – and men – are driven simply by the overwhelming physical desire to 'have another baby', and who knows, maybe scientists in the future will discover evolutionary reasons for this, a 'second child gene'. For many women, a second child is also a second chance, an opportunity to do things again and this time get it right. They find they are able to enjoy their second child's baby- and toddler-hood more than their first-born's because they are much more relaxed about everything. Other parents may be driven by peer pressure, or pressure from parents or grandparents. Deeper societal pressures are probably at work too: 'There may be a part of every parent-of-two, or three, or four, that fantasises about what life would have been like with a more manageable family structure,' argues Susan Maushart. 'But because this is a "dark wish" it makes us terribly uncomfortable and anxious. We banish the thought from consciousness and project it outwards as disapproval of others who have chosen the forbidden road. A couple who decide to limit their family to one child are regarded with as much suspicion as the voluntarily childless. When it comes to family density, two is definitely – in our society – the right way.'

For most of us, I suspect, the reasons, whatever they may be, remain tucked away in our subconscious, leaving us with no clearer explanation for the eventual size of our families than that we 'wanted two' – or maybe just 'wanted to'. And isn't there something rather magnificent about this flying in the face of reason, this stubborn, reckless desire to procreate, to take risks, to hope? Seen from this angle, every second child is a victory or, as Dr Johnson once said of second marriages, a triumph of hope over experience.

Being a mother to two children is not just a repeat of being a mother to one. From conception on, the experience is significantly different. Pregnancy is different, labour is different, recovery after labour is different. We have to adjust to loving two children, to caring for two children, and we must enable our children to love and care for one another. Becoming a mother-of-two impacts on the kind of parent we are, but also on the kind of partner we are. It changes our sense of who we are in relation to the world outside our homes, to the people inside it, and perhaps most importantly of all, it changes our sense of our self.

The transition from one child to two is as profound on an individual level as it is common on a social one. When the transition goes smoothly, there are ample rewards for the more difficult moments. When the transition does not go smoothly, the fall-out is felt by children, by adults, by couples, by communities, by employers, by society as a whole. If we could start to talk more honestly and openly about what the experience of parenting more than one child is really like, the experience could be made infinitely easier, less stressful, less guilt-ridden, with very real benefits for all.

There will always be someone who is ready to tell you that it's much easier second time round. And it's true – for *some* people, it is. But as with all these things, those who find it easier second time round spend a lot of time saying so, while the rest of us just keep quiet. The rule is universal and applies equally to how quickly you conceive (the one-shot wonders can't stop telling everyone); how well your children sleep (the straight-through-the nighters can't help gloating); how often you have sex (so how often do you have sex?), and how readily you cede your own needs to those of your offspring (needs? what needs?). The truth of the matter is that for some women having two children is a relatively effortless shift from having one child, while for others it is one of the biggest challenges they will ever face.

A wise old lady I know once told me that when you internalise problems, you become paranoid, when you externalise them, you become political. When it comes to bringing up children, it is easy to internalise problems, to see them as signs of our own personal failure, but it is just as likely, probably much more likely, that the problems are created by external circumstances. Next time you have a bloody awful time trying to get two children, a buggy and four carrier bags round your local shopping centre, and then get a parking fine for arriving back at your car after the ticket ran out, don't berate yourself for being an incompetent, disorganised wreck. Blame the council for failing to pedestrianise the city centre, blame the architects who design shops that are utterly unsuited to the needs of women with buggies and small children, blame the bus companies for still being impossible to board safely or easily with children in tow, blame the people who design buggies with nowhere to put the shopping. Channel your frustration into a stinging letter to the council, the buggy company, or your local MP.

Life for mothers of small children is not made any easier by the child-unfriendly society we are trying to do that caring in – which makes it mother-unfriendly too. Why do so few shops, banks, cafés and supermarkets have enclosed, supervised play-spaces where children can be happily and safely occupied while their parents go about their errands? Why do so few public lavatories have toilets and basins at child height? Why are pushchairs not designed so that an older child can stand behind, while the younger one sits in front? Small children turn us all into bag ladies, so why is there so little provision on buses and trains for the nappies, toys, clothes and refreshments that accompany us on even the most routine outing? And why aren't all forms of public transport fitted with safety belts for children under five?

The Joys of Two

This book began with the words of parents themselves and it seems right that it should end with their words too:

'It's a love affair, isn't it? It's just being with someone you love. They come into the room, and it lights up.'

'When they're little, you just can't take your eyes off them, they're so gorgeous. And it's being loved too. You know there are these two people who just adore you, who are always pleased to see you.'

'I like the sense of my children being envoys for me in the world, the feeling that they represent me, or part of me. I find it very fulfilling taking them to see my parents, for example. It's like taking a present with me, sharing something of myself. It's a way of giving something back to them.'

'The children bring a lot of happiness into our lives. They always have done, right from when they were tiny babies. They're always making us laugh with the things they say or do. I think people who don't have children miss out on all that, though they don't know it.'

'I love the deep sense of companionability. I took my children into town the other day and we were just pottering round the shops, running errands, then we had lunch in a café and came home. It was so lovely, being together, enjoying each other's company. We weren't doing anything special, but just being together like that made it special.'

'Seeing the relationship between them is wonderful. Even on the most humdrum days, I'll see them playing together and it's like the best feeling you can have as a parent.'

'It's their bodies! They're so beautiful, and soft, and warm. And when they put their arms round your neck, or their cheek against yours, it's just heaven really!'

'For me it's the awe-and-wonder thing. Children just bring you back to realising how incredible life is. It's also hard work and horrible! But my children never cease to amaze me with the things they say. It's to do with the way they see the world. They don't take any of it for granted. Children are very grounding in the best possible way.'

'My children give me a sense of life continuing beyond death, of life being bigger than just a person's life span. Our children are our future, aren't they?'

In her challenging and impassioned book, *Children First*, Penelope Leach lists several ways in which everyday life could be made safer and easier for children and their parents, as well as vastly more enjoyable: under-fives enclosures in every open space; dogs on leashes in parks; one-metre-high viewing slots on railway bridges and building sites; low slots on letter boxes; places for men to take their daughters to pee; supermarket check-outs for people with under-fives; play-coaches on all trains; special queues at post-offices and banks to enable people with small children to get served sooner. As Leach says, 'There are better choices for children available to us. We are not making them because we are not seeing them. We are not seeing them because we are not looking.'[4] According to Leach, instead of regarding children as a public nuisance, we should be 'recognising children as young citizens and paying as much attention to their rights and opportunities as to those of adults'. This, she argues, would also bring parents' rights and responsibilities to the fore, to the benefit of both parents and children, and ultimately to the benefit of society as a whole.

Of course, the most enlightened society in the world can't make a two-year-old want to put his socks on if he doesn't want to, or find his missing shoe once he's got his socks on. Nothing and no one can take *all* the stress and strain out of everyday life with small children. Nor, of course, can anyone legislate for the pleasure, laughter and delight of life with those same small children.

It is easier by far to describe the difficulties of life with two children than it is to convey adequately the profound rewards of the experience. How can mere words ever do justice to the privilege of knowing our children; to the delight of loving and being loved by them; to the intoxicating smell of their soft, warm skin; to the easy companionship; the thrill of seeing the world through their eyes; the boundless humour, laughter and fun; the endless excuses to play; the gentle nudging to keep life's problems in perspective; the opportunity to put things right from our own childhoods; the challenge of trying to give them the best of us; the miracle of having created life, and the humbling experience of watching that life take on a shape entirely of its own?

Having two children brings huge rewards, as every mother-of-two knows, however harried and exhausted she may be, and they are as intricately woven into the tapestry of daily life as the problems. Loving and being loved by your second child is as precious a pleasure as it was with your first; the sense of wonderment as you watch their personality unfold and develop is just as intense second time round. The swell of tenderness at the sight of your first child sleeping peacefully is only equalled in this world by the tenderness you feel at the sight of your second child doing the same. Life increases in complexity with two children, certainly, but the pleasures increase too. When you hear them shrieking with laughter somewhere upstairs; when you see the older one standing up for the younger one in a playground dispute; when you see the little one spontaneously embrace the older one; when you see both their faces side by side alight with excitement as they fall on their stockings on Christmas morning – it is reward enough and more.

NOTES

INTRODUCTION

1 Judy Dunn, *From One Child to Two*, p.9

THE TRANSITION TO TWO

1 Penny Munn, 'Mothering More than One Child' in *Motherhood: Meanings, Practices and Ideologies*, p.167

2 Steve Biddulph, *Raising Boys*, p.97

3 Kate Figes, *Life After Birth*, p.49

4 Judy Dunn, op. cit., p.21

5 Carolyn Pape Cowan, 'Becoming Parents: What Has to Change for Couples?' in *Partners Becoming Parents*, p.137

LET'S GET PHYSICAL

1 Susan Maushart, *The Mask of Motherhood*, p.69

2 Vicki Iovine, *The Best Friend's Guide to Surviving the First Year of Motherhood*, p.195

3 Iovine, ibid, p.195

4 Robert Stewart, *The Second Child:Family Transition and Adjustment*, p.181

5 Christine MacArthur, Margo Lewis and George Knox, *Health After Childbirth*

6 Figes, op. cit., p.149

7 Figes, ibid, p.247

8 Daws, 'Post-natal Depression and the Family: Conversations that Go Awry' in *Post-natal Depression: Focus on a Neglected Issue*, p.14

9 Iovine, op. cit., p.190

10 MacArthur et al, op. cit., p.54

11 MacArthur et al, ibid, p.57

12 Daws, op. cit., p.14

13 Maushart, op. cit., p.120

14 Harriet Lerner, *The Dance of Deception: Pretending and Truth-telling in Women's Lives*, p.214

15 Maushart, op. cit., p.105

WAYS OF LOVING

1 Stewart, op. cit., *p.134*

2 Munn, op. cit., p.1

3 Munn, ibid, p.163

4 Martha Heineman Pieper and William J. Pieper, *Smart Love: The Compassionate Alternative to Discipline*, p.106

5 Pieper and Pieper, ibid, p.106

6 Rozsika Parker, *Torn in Two: The Experience of Maternal Ambivalence*, p.91

7 Parker, ibid, p.24

8 Figes, op. cit., p.96

9 Adrienne Rich, *Of Woman Born*, p.21–22

10 Penny Munn, op. cit., p.168

11 Kate Figes, op. cit, p.99

12 Susan Maushart, op. cit, p.29

TEA FOR THREE

1 Munn, op. cit., p.174

2 Dunn, op. cit., p.66

3 Dunn, ibid, p.63

4 Dunn, ibid, p.67

5 Dunn, ibid, p.67

6 Jayne Buxton, *Ending the Mother War*, p.167–8

7 Stewart, op. cit., p.134

8 Dunn, op. cit., p.95

9 Stewart, op. cit., p. 192

10 Munn, op. cit., p.167

11 Stewart, op. cit., p 134

12 Figes, ibid, pp.126–7

13 Munn, op. cit., p.166

SIBLINGS, RIVALS & FRIENDS

1 Iovine, op. cit., p.193

2 Dunn, op. cit., p.128

3 Dunn, ibid, p.128

4 Stewart, op. cit., p.188

5 Dunn, op. cit., p.134

6 Steve Biddulph, *The Secret of Happy Children*, p.58

7 Biddulph, ibid, pp.57–8

8 *Social Trends* 30

9 Gill Gorell Barnes, Paul Thompson, Gwyn Daniel and Natasha Burchardt, *Growing Up in Step-families*, p.127

10 Gorell Barnes et al., ibid, p.127

11 Adele Faber and Elaine Mazlish, *Siblings Without Rivalry*, p.141

12 Faber and Mazlish, ibid, p.190–1

ALL ABOUT US

1 Sarah Blaffer Hrdy, *Mother Nature*, p.540

2 Melissa Benn, *Madonna and Child: Towards a New Politics of Motherhood*, p.3

3 Rich, op. cit., p.31–2

4 Maureen Freely, *What About Us? An Open Letter to the Mothers Feminism Forgot*, p.214

5 Rich, op. cit., p.31

6 Maushart, op. cit., p.22

7 Maushart, ibid, p.143

8 Maushart, ibid, pp.206–7

9 Stewart, op. cit., p.142

10 Maushart, op. cit., p 112

11 Fiona Shaw, *Out of Me*, p.25

12 Figes, op. cit., p.39

13 Kate Figes, ibid, p.41

14 Rozsika Parker, op. cit., p.96

15 Ellen Galinsky, 'What Children Say About Working Parents', paper given at Parent Child 2000, London, 13 April 2000

16 Malcolm George, 'Post-natal Depression, Relationships and

Men' in *Post-natal depression: Focus on a Neglected Issue*, p.17
17 George, ibid, p.19
18 Philip Cowan, 'The Couple Relationship Style? Outcomes for Children from Birth to Six', paper given at Parent Child 2000, London, 14 April 2000
19 Maushart, op. cit., pp.216
20 *The Millennial Family*, National Family and Parenting Institute Survey, October 1999, p.4
21 Dr Gordon Harold in *Parents as Partners: How Marriages Affect Children* (ed. Jenny Reynolds), One Plus One Marriage and Partnership Research, forthcoming publication, April 2001
22 Bryan Rodgers and Jan Pryor *Divorce and Separation: The Outcomes for Children*, pp.41–2
23 Rodgers and Pryor, ibid, p.15
24 Anthony Clare, *On Men: Maculinity in Crisis*, p.100
25 Anthony Clare, ibid, p.215
26 Anthony Clare, ibid, pp.169–177
27 Anthony Clare, ibid, pp.175–177
28 Anthony Clare, ibid, pp.219
29 Jo Warin, Yvette Solomon, Charlie Lewis and Wendy Langford, *Fathers, Work and Family Life*, p.11

30 Jayne Buxton, op. cit., p.52–3
31 Elsa Ferri and Kate Smith, *Parenting in the 1990s*, p.42
32 Warin et al., op. cit., p.27–30
33 Robert Stewart, op. cit., p.133
34 Robert Stewart, ibid, p.141
35 Ben Summerskill, 'Daddy's Home', the *Observer*, 1 October 2000

BETWEEN A ROCK & A WORKPLACE

1 Susan Maushart, op. cit., p.207
2 Diane Houston and Gillian Marks, 'Employment Choices for Mothers of Pre-School Children' in ESRC *Future of Work* Research Project, 2000
3 Buxton, op. cit., pp.165–6
4 'Shift Parents', The Daycare Trust, September 2000
5 Penelope Leach, *Children First*, pp.247–8
6 Leach, ibid, p.143
7 Houston and Marks, Families and Work, report for The Women's Unit, The Cabinet Office, 2000
8 Houston and Marks, ibid
9 Ann Dally, *Inventing Motherhood: The Consequences of an Ideal*, p.179
10 Freely, op. cit., p.63
11 Freely, ibid, p.63

12 Maushart, op.cit., p.202

13 Blaffer Hrdy, op. cit., p.494

14 Clare, op. cit., p. 99

15 Suzanne Franks, *Having None of It: Women, Men and the Future of Work*, p.240

16 Maureen Freely, 'Parents Deserve More Help', the *Observer*, 1 October 2000

PERFECTING IMPERFECTION

1 Christina Hardyment, *Perfect Parents*, p.353

2 Iovine, op. cit., p.194

3 Bruno Bettelheim, *A Good Enough Parent*

4 Leach, op. cit., p.264

HELP & ADVICE

Association for Post-natal Illness (APNI) tel. 020 7386 0868; 25 Jerdan Place, London SW6 1BE. Provides support to mothers suffering from post-natal illness and aims to increase public awareness and encourage research into its cause and nature.

Child Psychotherapy Trust tel. 020 7485 5510; Star House, 104–108 Grafton Road, London NW5 4BD. Free helpline for parents to discuss problems with a child psychotherapist.

Cry-sis tel. 020 7404 5011; London WC1N 3XX. Phone counselling for parents with babies who won't sleep.

Fathers Direct tel. 020 7920 9291; enquiries@fathersdirect.com; Herald House, Lambs Passage, Bunhill Row, London EC1Y 8TQ. Information service to promote close and positive relationships between men and their children.

Gingerbread tel. 0800 018 4318 (helpline); www.gingerbread.org.uk; 16–17 Clerkenwell Close, London EC1R 0AN. Support for lone parents; free helpline; local self-help groups.

Home Start UK tel. 0116 233 9955; 2 Salisbury Road, Leicester, LE1 7QR. Free, confidential help for parents of under-fives; trained volunteers visit at home to provide support and company. Three hundred schemes nationwide.

Meet-A-Mum Association tel. 020 8768 0123 (helpline, 7–10pm); tel. 020 8771 5595. Support and counselling for mothers of young children. Runs daytime meetings, speaker events and one-to-one support.

NCT (National Childbirth Trust) tel. 020 8992 2616; www.nct-online.org; Alexandra House, Oldham Terrace, Acton, London, W3 6NH. Provides antenatal classes, breast-feeding counselling and post-natal support. Branches nationwide.

National Council for One-parent Families tel. 0800 018 5026 (general helpline Monday to Friday 9.15am–5.15pm; maintenance and money helpline

Monday and Friday 10.30am–1.30pm, Wednesday 3.00pm–6.00pm); www.oneparentfamilies.org.uk; 255 Kentish Town Road, London NW5 2LX. Provides information and advice for lone parents and their children.

National Parenting and Family Institute tel. 020 7424 3460; www.e-parents.org. Puts parents in touch with appropriate organisations. Website has wide range of information and advice for parents.

New Ways To Work tel. 020 7930 0093 (helpline); 309 Upper Street, London N1 2TY. Information and advice on issues related to family and work.

Newpin tel. 020 7703 6326; 35 Sutherland Square, Walworth, London SE17 3EE. Runs support services for parents and step-parents in London and Northern Ireland, including parenting classes for second-time parents. It also has a fathers' service, offering drop-in centre, evening talks and support groups.

Night Nannies tel. 020 7731 6168; fax 020 7610 9767. London-based company that provides nannies from 9.00pm–7.00am.

Parentline Plus tel. 0808 800 2222 (helpline); www.parentlineplus.org.uk; 520 Highgate Studios, 53–79 Highgate Road, London NW5 1TL. Free national helpline for parents and step-parents; also runs parenting courses nationwide and has a website and leaflets covering a range of parenting issues.

Parents At Work tel. 020 7628 2128 (helpline). Support and advice on legal and practical issue for working parents. Useful publications on family-friendly organisations and so on.

What About The Children (WATCH) tel. 01386 561635; www.whataboutthechildren.org.uk/watch; 60 Bridge Street, Pershore, WR10 1AX. Independent information about the emotional needs of children under three and clear authoritative leaflets.

Young Minds tel. 0800 018 2138. Free information service for parents worried about the emotional well-being of their children.

Select Bibliography

Argyle, Michael, *The Psychology of Happiness* (Routledge, 1986)

Benn, Melissa, *Madonna and Child: Towards a New Politics of Motherhood* (Vintage, 1999)

Bettelheim, Bruno, *A Good Enough Parent* (Thames and Hudson, 1987)

Biddulph, Steve, *The Secret of Happy Children: A Guide for Parents* (Thorsens, 1998)

Biddulph, Steve, *Raising Boys* (CelestialArts, California, 1998)

Blankenhorn, David, *Fatherless America* (Basic Books, New York, 1995)

Buxton, Jayne, *Ending the Mother War* (Macmillan, 1998)

Clare, Anthony, *On Men: Masculinity in Crisis* (Chatto and Windus, 2000)

Clulow, Christopher (ed.), *Partners Becoming Parents* (Sheldon Press, 1996)

Cowan, Carolyn Pape, and Cowan, Philip, *When Parents Become Partners: The Big Life Change for Couples* (Basic Books, New York, 1992)

Dalton, Katharina, with Holton, Wendy, *Depression After Childbirth* (Oxford University Press, 1980)

Dally, Ann, *Inventing Motherhood: The Consequences of an Ideal* (Burnett Books, 1982)

Dreikurs, Rudolf, *Children: The Challenge* (Plume, 1990)

Douglas, Jo, and Richman, Naomi, *Coping With Young Children* (Penguin, 1984)

Dunn, Judy, *From One Child To Two* (Fawcett Columbine, 1995)

Dunn, Judy, and Kendrick, C., *Siblings: Love, Envy and Understanding* (Harvard University Press, 1982)

Faber, Adele, and Mazlish, Elaine, *Siblings Without Rivalry* (Piccadilly Press, 1999)

Feinmann, Jane, *Surviving the Baby Blues* (Ward Lock, 1997)

Ferri, Elsa, and Smith, Kate, *Parenting in the 1990s* (Family Policy Studies Centre, 1996)

Figes, Kate, *Life After Birth: What Even Your Friends Won't Tell You About Motherhood* (Viking, 1998)

Franks, Suzanne, *Having None of It: Men, Women and the Future of Work* (Granta, 1999)

Freely, Maureen, *What About Us? An Open Letter to the Mothers Feminism Forgot* (Bloomsbury, 1995)

Galinsky, Ellen, *Ask the Children* (Morrow, 1999)

Gorell Barnes, Gill; Thompson, Paul; Daniel, Gwyn; and Burchardt, Natasha; *Growing Up in Step-families* (Clarendon Press, Oxford, 1998)

Hochschild, Arlie, *The Time Bind: When Work Becomes Home and Home Becomes Work* (New York, Henry Holt, 1997)

Hrdy, Sarah Blaffer, *Mother Nature: A History of Mothers, Infants, and Natural Selection* (Vintage, 2000)

Hardyment, Christina, *Perfect Parents: Baby-care Advice Past and Present* (Oxford University Press, 1995)

Hardyment, Christina, *The Future of the Family* (Phoenix, 1998)

Iovine, Vicki, *The Best Friends' Guide to Surviving the First Year of Motherhood* (Bloomsbury, 1999)

Leach, Penelope, *Children First: What We Must Do – And Are Not Doing – For Our Children Today* (Michael Joseph, 1994)

Leach, Penelope, *Your Baby and Child* (Penguin, 1998)

Lerner, Harriet, *The Dance of Deception: Pretending and Truth-telling in Women's Lives* (HarperCollins, 1993)

Lindenfield, Gael, *Confident Children* (Thorsens, 1994)

MacArthur, Christine; Lewis, Margo; and Knox, George; *Health After Childbirth* (HMSO, 1991)

Maushart, Susan, *The Mask of Motherhood* (River Oram, 1999)

Parker, Rozsika, *Torn in Two: The Experience of Maternal Ambivalence* (Virago, 1995)

Phoenix, Ann; Woollett, Ann; and Lloyd, Eva (eds); *Motherhood, Meanings, Practices and Ideologies* (Sage, 1991)

Pieper, Martha, and Pieper, William, *Smart Love: The Compassionate Alternative to Discipline* (Harvard Common Press, 1999)

Raskin, Valerie Davis, *When Words Are Not Enough* (Robinson Publishing Ltd, 1999)

Reynolds, Jenny (ed.), *Parents as Partners: How Marriages Affect Children* (One Plus One Marriage and Partnership Research, 2001)

Rodgers, Bryan, and Pryor, Jan, *Divorce and Separation: The Outcomes for Children* (Joseph Rowntree Foundation, 1998)

Rich, Adrienne, *Of Woman Born: Motherhood as Experience and Institution* (Virago, 1977)

Shaw, Fiona, *Out of Me: The Story of a Post-natal Breakdown* (Viking, 1997)

Simpson, Helen, *Dear George* (Minerva, 1996)

Stewart, Robert, *The Second Child: Family Transition and Adjustment* (Sage, 1990)

Swiss, Deborah, and Walker, Judith, *Women and the Work/Family Dilemma: How Today's Professional Women are Finding Solutions* (John Wiley, New York, 1993)

Warin, Jo; Solomon, Yvette; Lewis, Charlie; and Langford, Wendy; *Fathers, Work and Family Life* (Family Policy Studies Centre, 1999)

INDEX

Acknowledgements

I am greatly indebted to all the women who over the past three years have so generously and honestly shared their experiences of becoming mothers-of-two, whether in private conversations, focus group discussions, recorded interviews or questionnaires. This book would have been immeasurably poorer without their contribution. Huge thanks, too, to Jacky Fleming, whose wonderful illustrations so exactly capture the spirit of the book.

I would also like to thank the many people whose professional expertise has enhanced these pages, and who in several cases made research findings available ahead of publication; in particular, Diane Houston; Katherine Rake; Alan Marsh; Hugh Davies; Christopher Clulow; Jenny Reynolds, Paul Eldrid; Brian Waller; Nicola Heathcote; Liz Bavidge; Shona Gore; Val Harris; Gael Lindenfield; and Rachel Oliver.

My agent, Georgina Capel, has provided a much appreciated flow of calm encouragement throughout the writing of this book, while John Mitchinson's enthusiastic and unwavering championing of the project as a whole has been completely invaluable. I am also grateful to Steve Guise at Cassell, who has been as thorough, attentive and diplomatic an editor as any author could hope for.

On a personal note, I wish to thank Buffy Slim; Margaret Stoton, Michael Holyoke, Catherine Clarke; Emily Cohen; Eluned Harris; Philippa Goodyer; Annabel Forestier-Walker; Catherine Carter; and Dr Ghazala Aziz-Scott, whose practical help and great kindness during my second pregnancy was deeply appreciated. I'd also like to thank Catherine and Michael for providing a quiet room and regular supplies of coffee when my own house was overrun with builders; John Slim for his news-cutting service – as crucial as ever; Kristy Ward for taking our family entirely in her stride and being such a great friend to the children; Cathy Troupp, Katie McLennan and Cath Lloyd for their helpful comments on early drafts of chapters; and for ploughing through the whole manuscript when you had a book of your own to finish, thank you, Ma!

Finally, and most of all, my heartfelt thanks to Hugo, for putting up with me not only finding having a second child so 'interstressting', but then having the bright idea of writing about it. And, of course, thanks to my precious, wonderful children, Jessica and Solomon, without whom absolutely none of this would have been written much sooner.

First published in the United Kingdom in 2001 by Cassell & Co

Reprinted March 2001

Text copyright © 2001 Rebecca Abrams
Design and layout copyright © 2001 Cassell & Co

A CIP catalogue record for this book is available from the British Library.

ISBN 0 304 35429 5

Designed by Austin Taylor
Cover illustration and cartoons by Jacky Fleming
'Three Shoes...' cover type by The Senate
Cover photograph by Nic Barlow

Printed and bound in Great Britain by Clays Ltd, St Ives plc

Cassell & Co
Wellington House
125 Strand
London WC2R 9BB